Celebrity
Passions

Now

First published in 2006 by IPC Connect,
a division of IPC Media/Time Warner

Now Magazine
King's Reach Tower
Stamford Street
London SE1 9LS
www.nowmagazine.co.uk

Editorial enquiries: 0207 261 5366
Email: nowletters@ipcmedia.com

Subscription enquiries: 0845 676 7778
Email: ipcsubs@qss-uk.com

© 2006 IPC Media Ltd

Photographs © Rex Features Ltd

Printed in the UK by Butler & Tanner

Distributed by:
Orca Book Services
Stanley House
3 Fleets Lane
Poole, Dorset
BH15 3AJ
01202 665432

ISBN 1 85277 526 2

ISBN 978 1 85277 526 1

Trade enquiries to: Chris Lynn, 020 7633 3450
Sales enquiries to: Phil Richards, 01299 402449
Email: magazinesales@ipcmedia.com

Introduction

For the last decade, *Now* magazine has been asking stars to list their passions. The answers have been surprising, heart-warming, often nostalgic, always revealing – and the end result is the most enduringly popular page in the UK's best-loved celebrity weekly.

We've had everything from Alicia Silverstone's fondness for teapots to Björk's taste for roast puffin. Moby describes how he delights in watching dogs in the park, Boy George admits a fondness for Marks & Spencer blazers and Jade Goody confesses to a crush on East 17's Brian Harvey.

Many passions come up time and time again – movies such as Pretty Woman and The Godfather, sushi, Italy, Marilyn Monroe and the TV series 24.

So what are the passions of your favourite celebrities? This great new book reveals the hidden depths – and sometimes the obvious shallows – of the men and women who dominate our celebrity-obsessed culture.

Jane Ennis, **Editor of *Now***

Renée Zellweger

Actress Renée adores collecting old books from junk shops and reading African-American literature

Mango's got to be one of my favourite afternoon snacks. I love the fresh packs you can buy in Marks & Spencer – they taste awesome. They don't tend to sell fresh fruit like that in the US, but I definitely think they should start.

I couldn't survive without my breakfast burrito every morning. I know it's really boring, but I'm addicted to them. I fill them with egg whites and just one can keep me going until lunchtime.

Being at my farm in Connecticut is the best holiday for me. I spend so much time travelling the world, there's no better feeling than walking through the door of my own house. I feel so relaxed when I'm there.

Cats are such fascinating animals. I admire the way they are so independent and self-sufficient. What I really love about them is that they all have their own personalities.

I love my job and I love what it brings. The best thing about it is that it exposes me to things that I wouldn't otherwise have a reason to see and explore. I'm just so lucky to learn and see new things all the time. I'm becoming a better person because of my job and that is such a gift.

My main passion on TV is the news. Wherever I am in the world, I always watch the local news. It's so interesting to see what the top stories are in different countries.

Oscar Wilde would be my perfect dinner date. I've always had an appreciation for his work and I think he was very handsome. He'd give the most fascinating advice on life.

Tom Cruise is the most genuine person in the industry. He never runs out of energy and I applaud him for that. He has time for everyone, whether they're a waitress or a movie star. It takes a lot to be like that.

I love old, beautiful books. The best feeling is accidentally finding a first edition in an old junk shop. Whatever the title, I'd buy it. I've got quite an impressive collection. I like African-American literature because of its musicality and its history. There is a depth to it.

Jamie Oliver

The celebrity chef and TV star, who was awarded an MBE in 2003, loves The Killers, Paul Smith and the taste of paprika

Rome is gorgeous. Jools and I go there every year on our own and have some 'us' time. We love Spain, too, and at the Hotel La Residencia in Deia, Mallorca, we sat on the terrace overlooking the village, eating lobster with peaches. Genius.

I love food... well, most foods. Not bollocks and brains – I got some of that in Japan – but I enjoy almost anything. It just depends on how you cook it! Fish pie is a favourite – it all goes back to my childhood.

Paul Smith is my favourite designer. It's not just the cut of his clothes, it's the details of his designs. All the little extras – the buttons and things. He's great.

I sold my scooter on Ebay for £7,600. It's about getting old! My fave mode of transport is my 1956 VW Camper. And it's still going...

Barbecues are great because they're the most basic method of cooking. I think cooking with wood is beautiful because it gives food loads of flavour. What's so good is that, in the last few years, the grills in many restaurants have changed from being gas fired to either charcoal or wood ovens, so you get all that fabulous extra flavour.

Gordon Ramsay's a really good bloke. He's funny, bright and sticks to his guns. He has his own individual style, which is totally not my style, but I completely respect it. He's very much grassroots French with a worldly English slant.

I'm a fan of Italian red wines. Ever since I was teenager, I've been besotted by the love, passion and verve for food, family and life that just about all Italians have, no matter where they're from or how rich or poor they might be.

The Killers and Keane are bloody good. They are among my favourite bands. I don't drum with my band Scarlet Division any more, but I am still passionate about my music.

My favourite ingredient is paprika. I love everything about it – the strong smell, the spicy flavour, the rich taste and the texture. It goes with absolutely everything.

Susan Sarandon

Susan enjoys eating a plate of oysters, drinking espresso and visiting Italy with her family, especially the city of Rome

I'm a passionate lover of seafood. You can't beat a plate of wonderful oysters. They have to be fresh, though – preferably caught on the same day that you eat them.

My idea of fun has to be dancing round the living room with my children doing the dance moves from Grease. It's such a great soundtrack to a great movie. Sometimes Tim walks in right in the middle of a big number – he probably thinks we're all crazy!

I used to live in Rome and I absolutely love the city, especially the Colosseum, which I enjoy visiting with my kids. The Sistine Chapel is also well worth a visit, but really you could say that about all the individual beautiful little squares that can be found all over the city.

Before acting alongside Geoffrey Rush in The Banger Sisters, I had no idea just what a great actor he is. I'd only seen him do straight drama before, but he's a fantastic comedic actor with a wonderful sense of humour. I presented him with his Best Actor Oscar in 1996.

Being from New Jersey, my musical hero is the great Bruce Springsteen, whom I'm also fortunate enough to call a friend. I love the fact that his music keeps evolving and stays fresh. He's certainly one of the great songwriters of our age. A good sense of humour and a great brain mean a lot to me – and Bruce has both.

I always used my ever-reliable Volvo to drive my kids to school every morning. I try to be a normal mother who does the family chores. In fact, I'm one of nine children myself.

I'm really fascinated by all aspects of Indian culture, especially the life of Gandhi. I remember when my husband Tim was filming in India some time ago – I couldn't wait to see what presents he would bring back for me.

There's nothing quite like a steaming hot cup of espresso to get your day going. Some mornings, I'm sure it's the only thing in the world that will get me out of my bed. It's a great way to start the day. I don't know what I'd do without it.

Lenny Kravitz

Lenny is good friends with Gene Simmons, treasures his Harley-Davidson and has always been a huge fan of Aretha Franklin

As a kid I remember watching Born Free, a TV show about lions that I'd never miss. It had a great title song sung by Matt Monro and I can recall being at my grandma's house when I was about two, playing that record over and over...

Home to me is in the Bahamas because that's where my family comes from. I once spent five months there, which is a very long time for me to be staying in one place. I love relaxing and playing guitar with the local guys at this little wood-shack bar.

I remember going to see Aretha Franklin sing at the New Orleans Jazz Festival. I was totally blown away by her voice. I don't think you'll ever find a voice like hers that is so pure and full of soul. I would drink her bath water.

I try to stick to my macrobiotic diet. The diet consists of eating the purest and most nutritious natural foodstuffs prepared in the healthiest way possible. One of my favourite macrobiotic dishes is definitely lobster, which I eat regularly.

When I was a kid in New York, I was really into Kiss. You could probably guess that by some of the clothes I wear, although I've never done that face paint thing! I've seen them play live many times. Lead singer Gene Simmons is a real hero of mine and a good friend.

Stanley Kubrick was a genius whose films will be remembered as classics for ever. It was unfortunate and ironic that he died just a few days after he finished Eyes Wide Shut. 2001: A Space Odyssey is my favourite film that he directed.

I love getting on my Harley-Davidson motorcycle and just forgetting about the music business. When I get out there on the highway, I feel so free because there's no phone, no fax and no one can bother you. It's just me and the wide open road.

I've always been a big fan of Antoni Gaudi's architecture. I especially admire the work he did in Barcelona. One day I would love to build a Gaudi-style house right in the middle of the jungle.

Amanda Holden

Amanda wants Abba's Dancing Queen to be played at her funeral and has a bit of a thing about Jack Nicholson

My favourite group's always been Abba. When I was small, I had a pink blanket with Disco Queen written on it, which I'd wear round my shoulders while listening to Dancing Queen. I want that song played at my funeral.

I love the TV series Porridge and I've seen all the episodes many times over. The on-screen chemistry between Ronnie Barker and Richard Beckinsale is wonderful to watch.

There's nothing nicer than relaxing with a gin and tonic with lots of ice, while lying back in a hot tub. To complete the mood, you just need some scented candles and bath potions.

I couldn't stand Kilroy when he was on TV because Robert Kilroy is the most patronising git ever. I can't abide seeing people like him because they're so self-righteous.

I have a lot of friends in Norfolk and I often go there just to chill out for a while on the Broads. I've been going for years and I've really fallen in love with the whole county – it's such a beautiful place.

Cate Blanchett is a heroine of mine. As an actress, she has this wonderful ability to take on vastly different roles from different periods of history and make them believable.

London really is the greatest city in the world, even though people tend to complain about the crime levels and pollution. It's best to forget all that and enjoy its incredibly diverse culture.

I'm addicted to Desperate Housewives. People have slagged off the second series, but I thought it was just as gripping as the first. It's real black comedy and totally off-the-wall. I'd love to appear in an episode.

Jack Nicholson is fantastically charismatic, with such a naughty look in his eye. He never seems to lose that killer charm with the girls, despite getting older.

A Prayer For Owen Meany has to be my favourite book of all time. I've read it at least five or six times at different points in my life and it just gets better and better. I think everyone should read it!

Eric McCormack

Will & Grace star Eric loves Queen's late, great Freddie Mercury, penning tunes with Barry Manilow, eating in Italy and drinking lager

One of my favourite books is Easy Riders, Raging Bulls by Peter Biskind. It's really interesting. The 70s is my favourite period for movies and it was enthralling to find out what the people I watched on screen were really up to.

I love a nice glass of beer – it's just a shame it's so fattening. When I was younger, my favourite drink was lager and lime.

Woody Allen is the best film-maker around and Annie Hall is my favourite film. I was about 12 when I discovered him. I loved that urban Jewish humour of his, despite the fact that I'm not Jewish and I didn't grow up in New York.

The most exciting place I've ever visited is Tuscany in Italy. It has a perfect laid-back feel to it and the food and drink are amazing. I love the way people appreciate meal times far more than back in the US.

Composing a song with Barry Manilow for a Will & Grace album was a dream come true. He'd guested on our show, so I approached him to see if he would help me. Next thing, I was in a studio singing, with him accompanying me.

I grew up in Vancouver in Canada and I think it's one of the most amazing cities in the world. I now live mainly in LA because of work, but I spend a lot of time in Vancouver.

You can't beat a nice steak. My favourite type of steak has to be filet mignon, cooked medium rare – if I'm being fussy that is!

When I was a kid, I loved Freddie Mercury and my favourite band was Queen. It's so sad that he's no longer with us – I would've loved to have had the chance to meet him.

The best smell in the world is my son Finnegan right after he's had a bath. I love being a father and my son's just the best thing that's ever happened to me.

It's not on TV any more, but in its heyday the sitcom Seinfeld was so funny. It always cracked me up. Most of the TV I watch these days is what my young son wants to watch.

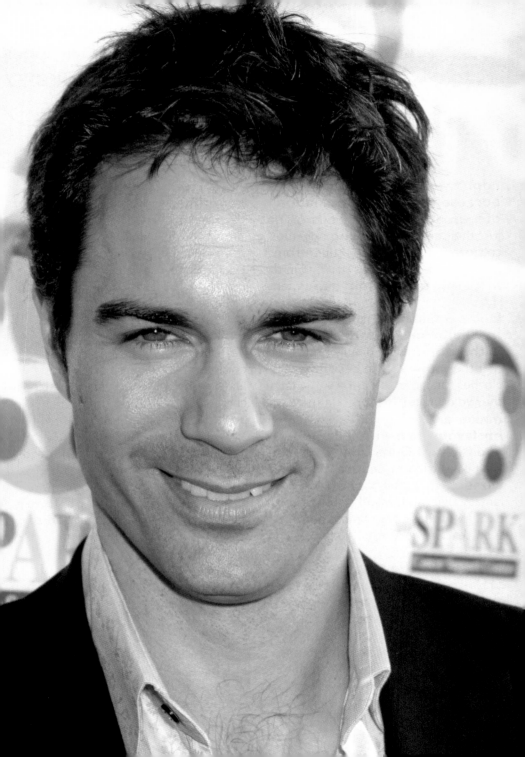

Anastacia, who battled breast cancer in 2003, hasn't needed her beloved trademark specs since she had laser eye surgery

Anastacia

I don't wear a particular perfume because I prefer a combination of aromatherapy body oils. It's not just their aroma – they also help me to sleep better because I suffer from insomnia. The perfumes you find in the shops have too much alcohol in them.

Dolce & Gabbana make the most fabulous designer clothes in the world. I feel deeply honoured that they now want to design stage clothes for me in the same way that they've done for Madonna in the past.

Pretty Woman with Julia Roberts and Richard Gere is my favourite film of all time because it's so wonderful. It's full of a kind of fantasy that Hollywood doesn't do enough of these days. I must have seen that movie at least 10 times.

Spectacles have always played a major role in my life. I used to be obsessed with checking out the weird frames at my local opticians. I'd say to my mum: 'Can I have the ones with the windshield wipers on or the ones with the big jewels glittering on them?' I own over 20 pairs now and have spent a fortune on them.

Paris is definitely the most beautiful city in the world. I only discovered Europe a few years ago, but now I've fallen in love with all things French – especially the capital. I could see myself living there one day.

I really love sushi – indeed any food of Asian origin. I think their food preparation is just so much healthier. When I'm at home, it's a completely different matter, though. I prefer simple food. I really like to chow down on chicken, mashed potatoes and corn.

My favourite drink is a mix of Sambuca and Bailey's on the rocks. Not a popular combination in the UK? Give it a try – you'll love it. Failing that, an awesome full-bodied red wine is fantastic.

I've always been a huge fan of Elton John. I couldn't believe it when he gave my album a wicked review in The Paper, a trendy New York magazine. When I sang Saturday Night's Alright (For Fighting) on stage with him during his concert at Madison Square Garden, it was the best night of my life.

Boris Becker

When he's not sunning himself or watching comedy, former Wimbledon champion Boris enjoys seeing Al Pacino in gangster movies

I enjoy watching American comedians. I like to go and see Eddie Murphy, but my favourite now is Chris Rock. He's a very funny man who uses language really cleverly.

I've been collecting watches ever since I was 16. I've got ones by Rolex and Cartier, but for me the best watches are IWC from Switzerland.

Cars are my thing and I'm a big Mercedes fan. The Mercedes SLR is probably the finest sports car in the world – I love it.

My favourite food is definitely Italian. I like everything from tomato and mozzarella salad to spaghetti. The best place to eat Italian food these days is in London.

I like hot weather and I'm a big fan of the sun and beaches. Miami Beach is a great resort. I have a holiday home in Miami, so I get to spend quite a bit of time there enjoying the sun.

Muhammad Ali is the greatest sportsman of all time. He's my all-time hero because his influence extended beyond sport. He's a man who was prepared to stand up for what he believed in, no matter what the cost. He's an iconic figure and will be remembered for years.

The novel I couldn't put down was The Da Vinci Code by Dan Brown. I like the way it's supposed to be fiction, yet makes you feel it could be true. I like a book that can play with your imagination and keeps you guessing.

I really love gangster movies. As well as exciting, I find them quite funny. The Godfather films are my favourites because they've also got great actors. Marlon Brando, Robert De Niro and Al Pacino are all amazing at what they do.

Ask any German about beer and you'll have a long conversation. If I'm in a bar, I've got to have a beer. I like them all, but my favourite is a Czech one called Pilsner Urquell.

My musical tastes have changed a lot over the years. But the one band I've always come back to for 25 years is U2. I can always listen to them and never get tired of their lyrics.

Charlotte Church

Welsh songbird and child star Charlotte had a No2 hit with her first pop single Crazy Chick

I love being Welsh – I think it's great that we all sing and play rugby. I'm really patriotic. I just think we're more passionate than other nations. We've got a proper identity. Our accent is wonderful.

My boyfriend Gavin [Henson] and I are DVD addicts. No matter how stressed you are in daily life, a DVD is escapism and you lose yourself for a couple of hours.

My new vice is McDonald's Sweet Chilli Chicken Baguette. I usually cook every night, but if I'm running late, then I grab one on the way home.

If I could do anything differently, I'd have worked with Daniel Bedingfield. I've always loved his stuff, although I hear he's a bit of an eccentric character.

My new house is lush – I designed it myself. I've got an ethnic-style living room with underfloor heating, dark leather sofas and bamboo wallpaper. The dining room is black lacquered furniture and my bedroom has gorgeous saris everywhere.

Lee Evans is just fab. I saw him in concert in Cardiff and he was brilliant. I don't think he's sexy, but he's very funny on stage.

Every woman should read The Memoirs Of Cleopatra by Margaret George. It's fabulous. When I finished it, I just wanted to cry. I read about two books a week.

Strawberry Ribena is delicious. I'll drink it all day if it's there. It's my only diva-esque demand.

I really love cooking. I'm a proud housewife. I recently cooked a big leg of lamb with rosemary and coated it in honey – it was fabulous. I watch all the TV cookery shows.

I sometimes decide to eat healthily. If I do, I always ask for slices of Parma ham and usually just eat it neat.

I think the smoking ban is a really good idea. A lot of social smokers never smoke during the week, just at the weekend, and they won't be able to soon. It's a much nicer atmosphere without smoke.

Lionel Richie

Singer Lionel loves visiting London, the smell of lavender, tennis matches at Wimbledon and spending time with his faithful dog Clyde

I'm a big fan of Elvis Presley's music and his Love Me Tender single was the first record I ever bought. I was about nine years old at the time and the record shop was right next door to my house. It only cost me 50 cents.

I'm a big tennis fan. I used to play every day, but I don't play much any more. I was once very good, but I'm nothing to brag about these days. I'm completely fascinated by Wimbledon – I watch it religiously, as well as all the other tournaments.

Magic Johnson is a brilliant athlete. I've had the pleasure of watching him at the height of his career and saw him go through his ups and downs. He's done wonders for basketball and no one else came close to achieving the success that he's had.

I love London. It reminds me of New York and I call it Europe's melting pot. It has so many different cultures and influences. I first visited in 1971 and played a gig at Ronnie Scott's jazz club. I was amazed at the eclectic group of people we attracted and it had a lasting impression on me.

Raging Bull is my favourite film, which is weird because it's crude and rude. But I still think it's great. I've watched it at least 14 times. It's not a pretty film, but artistically speaking it's fantastic. It's really gritty.

Dogs are man's best friend and my cocker spaniel Clyde is the only one who understands me. He's the epitome of loyalty. When I'm at the recording studio at 4am and everyone has gone to bed, the only one still with me is Clyde.

Sidney Poitier is one of my favourite actors. I'm honoured to be able to call him my friend and mentor. He's a man of such elegance and eloquence. His delivery and his demeanour are things you can't replace. He's just so smooth.

Lavender is a great smell and I mix it with frankincense to create the most gorgeous scent. I use it instead of aftershave because I hate the idea of smelling like someone else. I find it freaky when you can identify what a person is wearing. It's my quest to be an individual, so I like mixing essential oils together.

I love Issey Miyake's designs, but you have to take special care of his creations. A few years ago, I took a £2,000 dress of his to my dry-cleaner and they ironed the theatrical crimps by mistake. When I picked it up, it looked like an expensive nightie.

I'm still a huge fan of British club and DJ culture. Sometimes, though, you have to visit 50 clubs, then, at number 51, if you're still there at six in the morning, you'll see miracles. It's a question of mind over matter and everything's possible.

I see my Chinese medicine doctor at the Good Health Clinic in London at least once a week. Of all the treatments I've tried, acupuncture is my favourite. It's all about balancing out the yin and yang. To strengthen my lungs, I have needles inserted on the area of skin between my thumb and forefinger.

It's interesting to try unusual food and eating puffin is an enjoyable alternative in Iceland. Puffin meat is quite tough and very dark. British people think you may as well have come from Mars if you eat roast puffin, but you lot eat pigeons, sparrows and ducks.

I adore Istanbul, although the coffee they drink there really makes you buzz. After a few cups once I was so hyper, I walked all the way to Asia (from the European part of the city).

I miss the optimistic Icelandic way of drinking. If an Icelander loses a leg, we say, 'Oh, well, it got in the way of the other leg anyway.' We lived in mud houses until the early part of the 20th century, with hard winters, Danish oppression, no animals and high taxes. So we're very extreme and we never drink in moderation.

I enjoy watching documentaries about wildlife and the planet. David Attenborough is my biggest inspiration. One of the joys of living in London when my son Sindri was younger was the Natural History Museum. He adored the dinosaurs.

At seven, I was obsessed with the band Sparks. I thought the Mael brothers looked very oriental and theatrical when they performed.

Boy George

George O'Dowd enjoys TV hit classic Dynasty, looks up to Joan Collins and enjoys vegetarian food, especially cheese and onion sandwiches

I'm not a designer freak. I prefer practical places such as Marks & Spencer. It's a great shop to buy blazers from. I'll take them home and get out the sequins and paint to turn them into the kind of creations that no one else will have.

I used to have such a crush on Shakin' Stevens. I loved his 50s look and he was quite sexy. My band Culture Club only got on Top Of The Pops the first time because he was too ill to perform. So thanks, Shaky – you made us!

Vodka and cranberry juice is my favourite drink. I'm currently living in New York and the bartenders here like to serve them really strong. They'll just slosh in the vodka and, because it's not measured, you get so drunk. It's like drinking petrol.

From the age of 11, Top Of The Pops was the centre of my universe. Every Thursday night I used to watch bands like T Rex and dream of being part of their fantastic, glittering bohemian world. Woe betide if I ever upset my father and he wouldn't let me watch it.

Russia's an overwhelming country. I'm not bothered about sitting on a beach and getting a suntan – I'd rather go on holiday to a place like Moscow. It's culturally very interesting and the guys there are pretty cute, too!

I've always looked up to strong women like Joan Collins. In Dynasty, she played Alexis Colby, a complete bitch who got whatever she wanted. Her whole look screamed out 'camp'.

Archbishop Desmond Tutu is very open-minded. He's one of the few religious people I've ever heard say anything good about gay people. I've got a lot of respect for him.

Nothing beats the simplicity of a cheese and onion sandwich. It's delicious made with crusty bread and sharp Cheddar. If you're feeling sorry for yourself, it's great comfort food.

I love religious paraphernalia, whatever the denomination. I've got 10 Buddha statues in my house, all in the front room. My hallway's full of Christian artefacts.

28

Caprice Bourret

Caprice grew up in California, is a secret heavy metal fan and admires the beauty of Audrey Hepburn

I love yellow roses – and I think the word has got out that I adore them! With any other type of flowers I suffer from really bad hay fever, but with yellow roses for some reason I'm A-OK. So feel free to keep on sending them, please.

I absolutely loved my Mercedes SLK 230 Kompressor because it was small, compact and reliable, and I bought it for a very good price. It wasn't exactly a soft top, but you could press this little button and the top went down.

I'm a huge fan of Val Kilmer – he's fantastic. He has a reputation for being a difficult actor, but I think it's because he immerses himself so completely in his roles, like the time he played Jim Morrison in Oliver Stone's The Doors.

If I could be any film actress, I would be Audrey Hepburn. I absolutely loved her in Breakfast At Tiffany's and in Sabrina. She's a classic beauty icon, very sexy in an innocent sort of way, which makes her appealing. I think it's difficult to find that kind of personality these days.

You may not believe me, but I've always loved AC/DC. And whenever I hear Back In Black, which is my favourite track, I turn into a headbanging rocker.

Will Smith is a wonderful talent. He can dance, he can sing, he can act. The man is very sexy, with a very good body, a beautiful smile and a very, very big talent. I've never met him, but he seems really approachable.

Out of all the actors who've played James Bond, Sean Connery has always been my favourite. He's tall, good looking, suave and charismatic. Oh, and he's got a sexy voice, too.

Clinique Happy has to be one of my favourite perfumes. It's lovely and works well on my skin, staying on all day. For once, I think the name reflects the smell.

The K-Club in Barbuda, which is in the Caribbean, is my favourite place in the world to chill out in. I've seen quite a few exotic places while working on my cable TV travel show, but this is by far the coolest.

Robbie Coltrane

Born Anthony Robert McMillan, the Cracker star lives in a farmhouse in Scotland and likes to collect vintage cars

Phil Silvers was the greatest American comic and I can recite most of the Bilko scripts by heart. Like our own Tony Hancock, he had such an incredible sense of timing and the kind of face that begged you to laugh.

Scotland is great for salmon fishing. The best way to do it is to pull them out of the water and cook them on the spot.

I'm into Country and Western, especially at the Grand Ole Opry in Glasgow on a Saturday night – great for a bit of a bop. I could listen to jazz music all day. I'm a huge fan of John Coltrane, from whom I took my surname.

Growing up in Glasgow meant I connected with the gritty reality of the film Mean Streets. It starred two of my favourite actors, Robert De Niro and Harvey Keitel. I saw it 18 times and then I knew I wanted to act.

I've always loved books about real crime because my dad was a police surgeon. There's a bloke called Professor Glaister and his books about criminal toxicology are fascinating, just so long as you don't look at the pictures because they are rather horrifying.

Grolsch is my favourite beer. A friend used to bring me back a crate whenever she went to Holland.

I restore vintage cars and my pride and joy is a 1956 Coupe DeVille. I also have a 1981 Checker, which I think is the last ever built.

Cooking is a real passion and a first-class meal should finish with lots of Scottish Cheddar. I taped a Madhur Jaffrey TV series and ruined my VCR. I'd run back in from the kitchen and press 'play' for the next bit of the recipe. It was covered in curry for weeks.

Driving across America, I fell in love with the sight and sweet smell of the Joshua trees in the Nevada Desert. When I was growing up, I had these cowboy boots with an illustration of a cactus and one of those wonderful, electric-red skies mellowing into yellow and then blue on the side of them.

Carol Vorderman

Carol collects everything from sets of scales to computers and hopes they're a good investment

I'm an avid collector of weighing scales. It started years ago when Mum brought home lots of weights and scales from an old science block she worked in as a school secretary. I also collect mobile phones and computers. They date so quickly, they'll soon become collectables.

Chess is a great way to relax and no game's ever the same as another. I got interested while hosting a TV series involving world champion Gary Kasparov. I wouldn't say I'm that good, but it's a marvellous game of strategy and skill.

Victoria Wood is one of the funniest people around. She is very witty and perceptive and the only woman to make me laugh out loud. I'm one of those sad people who can recite some of her stories and jokes word for word.

A Jaguar XJ8 is perfection itself. It's a beautiful drive, really comfortable with a nice bit of oomph. I did a lot of miles in one and it got me everywhere without leaving me feeling exhausted. It also brought a few admiring glances – and I never mind that.

I loved the sitcom Frasier. The timing of the actors was brilliant, especially Niles, who was the real star of the series. Like Frasier himself in Cheers, Niles was a character who could have had his own show.

I like The Undertones and once made a cover version of their hit Teenage Kicks. I was in a pop band called Dawn Chorus And The Blue Tits until my mother pointed out that we'd never be taken seriously. But I'd love to have been in a group like the Spice Girls. I'd have been Sums Spice.

Disney's Snow White And The Seven Dwarfs is magical – it reminds me of my childhood. I watched it with my daughter Katie, but we had to forward the bit where the wicked stepmother turns into a witch because it was too frightening.

I used to marshal at stock-car races and rallies and I adore Formula One. It's a fantasy of mine to get behind the wheel of a car and really give it some welly. My brother was a stock-car racer and our back yard was always littered with bits of engine waiting to be rebuilt.

Uri Geller

Uri Geller discovered his spoon-bending powers in his native Israel at the age of four and wishes he could fly. He'd like to be reborn as a kingfisher

My life is great and I wouldn't want to be any other person. But I'd love to be able to fly. It's my dream to flap my arms and take off. I believe in reincarnation and pray I'll come back as a kingfisher.

One of my greatest wishes was to appear on Friends. Ross's surname is Geller – I thought I could appear as one of his relatives.

Nothing is more important to me than feeling at peace. The most peaceful spot in the world is the extinct volcano Mount Fujiyama. It's incredibly spiritual, very quiet and green with a snow-capped cone. I did a show in Japan in 1973 and used the money I earned to buy a bungalow there, which I've had ever since.

I always carry a bottle of Old Spice aftershave in the glove compartment of my car. That for me is an absolute classic. It always smells good and triggers happy memories of when I first wore it in the 60s. And I can't live without the smell of lavender. An Italian countess gave me a sack of it 30 years or so ago, though I didn't like to ask why.

I love pop music. The Spice Girls and East 17 were big favourites and I'm a huge fan of Streisand. The ones I'm really hot on are an American rock band called Toad The Wet Sprocket, mainly because they mention me in a song. The line goes: 'You bend my words like Uri Geller bends his spoons.' Great.

The books that really touch me are ones about people who've dared to live their dreams. A real inspiration is Captain Edgar Mitchell's The Way Of The Explorer. Mitchell was on Apollo 14 and was the sixth man to walk on the moon. I met him once and made a tiepin he'd lost on a beach five years earlier reappear for him in an ice cream he was eating. He was very shocked.

My favourite place in the world is my conservatory at home. I've got an exercise bike there and rock crystals. The best bit is the floor – it's 500 million years old. I had it made from tiles cut out of fossils from a German quarry. There are also plants in it that date back to prehistoric times. It's beautiful and I love spending time in there relaxing.

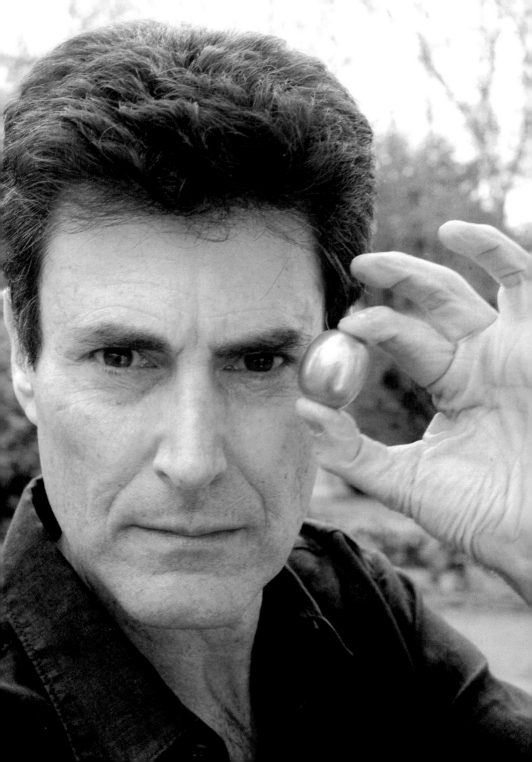

Davina McCall

Big Brother host Davina likes a glass of elderflower champagne while she sits back to watch her favourite black and white movie

My favourite plant is the frangipani. I was out visiting family in Melbourne, Australia, when I first smelled one. I'd never come across such an amazing scent before and it's also a great name – anything called frangipani has got to be good.

The Maldives are by far the most beautiful place in the world. I went to Reethi Rah, which is one of the tinier islands. It was the most idyllic place for diving, snorkelling and looking at turtles.

I love science fiction and I'm a real Trekkie. My favourite Star Trek captain is Jean-Luc Picard. Patrick Stewart is just delicious.

I've worn Chanel No 19 all my life. Whenever I've strayed from it, I felt like I was being unfaithful. My mother gave me my first bottle when I was about 14. I put too much on and ended up really stinking the place out.

The Guggenheim Museum in Bilbao, Spain, is breathtaking – it has such a beautiful metallic rounded shape. Simple Minds used it in one of their videos. When the sun's shining, it looks just like one gigantic glitterball. Fantastic.

I cried with laughter the first time I saw Bringing Up Baby. It's an old black and white movie starring Katharine Hepburn and Cary Grant – and a leopard. Their relationship on film is just so funny. A friend said I'd love it and he was right. I bought the video the next day.

Elderflower champagne is so delicious – and alcohol-free. It's lovely without being too sickly sweet and it looks like you're having alcohol, so people don't give you a hard time for not drinking. It's absolutely perfect.

I never missed watching Tiswas on TV when I was growing up. Sally James looked so sexy in those tight waistcoats of hers. I used to think she was the funkiest old person I'd ever seen.

Chauffeur bikes are the best ever way of travelling. Everyone should use them. They're such a laugh, I'll never travel any other way – unless it's raining. It's like sitting in an armchair as you whizz through the traffic.

Caroline Quentin

Caroline Quentin loves nothing more than a good bottle of wine and taking baths scented with Chanel No5

I had six months off work after I gave birth to my daughter Emily in 2000 and ended up totally addicted to daytime TV talk shows. I tried not to, but I sat glued to Trisha, Vanessa, Kilroy – the lot. While watching them, I'd be thinking: 'This is crap,' but I couldn't move away. I'd even shout at Trisha!

To treat myself, I love relaxing in a hot bath with Chanel No5 in it. It's such a beautiful fragrance and, after a hard day's work, there's nothing nicer than allowing yourself a little luxury by having a hot bath.

I'm not exactly a label queen, but I do own a very expensive pair of high-heel Gucci shoes. I love to wear them when I'm going out somewhere nice. I do own more shoes than I probably need, but like most women, I can't bring myself to throw any of them out.

I've always had a real passion for drinking wine. A good bottle of either a full-bodied red or white is a great reason for staying in and relaxing in front of the TV with a box of chocolates and your feet up. Lovely.

I think Isabella Rossellini is incredibly beautiful. She looks fabulous for her age. As both an actress and a model, she continues to break down the barriers for women of a certain age.

I love The Seagull by Chekhov. He was a genius – a brilliant playwright and a practising doctor for over 10 years. He once said: 'Medicine is my legal spouse, while literature is my mistress. When I get tired of one, I go and sleep with the other.'

I used to like a cigarette, it has to be said. I gave up smoking when I knew I was expecting Emily, but the day after she was born, I said to myself: 'It's all right now, I'll have one.' I've since read a book on how to quit, but it's not as easy to give up as I thought it would be.

If I'm on a long journey, I like to flick through a copy of the magazine Garden Answers. I dream of turning my own back garden into one of those shown in one of their features. I think the English take great pride in their gardens – and I'm no exception.

Bryan Adams

Canadian-born Bryan Adams, who now lives in Chelsea, is biased about his choice of Bond girl and would love to live on a Jamaican beach

I live in Chelsea and I'm a very keen follower of the local football team. I think Ruud Gullit was probably the best player to ever wear the blue shirt. It was sad when he had to leave the club.

My favourite actress is Uma Thurman. She really did it for me in Pulp Fiction. Once I saw her sitting in a restaurant and I tripped up as I was going through the door. I made a complete fool of myself.

One of my favourite meals is just a basic baked potato and salad. A lovely dressing is fresh lime juice and extra virgin olive oil in equal amounts, with salt and pepper. It's the most yummy salad dressing you can make.

The Busabong Tree, a Thai restaurant right next to my London home, is where I really love to eat. The food is great and the cocktail list is pretty good, too.

I really liked Mel C right from the moment we met in a hotel lift in Los Angeles. We went to have a drink at the bar and it was then that I asked her if she'd like to do a duet with me. She said yes right away and we recorded Baby When You're Gone.

Jamaica is paradise on earth and I'd like to live there in a beach house. Jamaican people are so friendly and they love their music.

I'm a big fan of the Bond films, although I'm somewhat biased when choosing my favourite Bond girl. Professor Inga Bergstrom in Tomorrow Never Dies was played by my ex-girlfriend Cecile Thomsen.

Robert Downey Jr is my favourite actor. Like most geniuses, he's had his share of personal problems, but when you see him take on a character like Charlie Chaplin, you realise what a talent he is.

One of my ambitions has always been to sing with the great Luciano Pavarotti. I was fortunate enough to do a duet with him on the Italian folk song O Sole Mio in 1995. He makes great spaghetti, too.

I love having friends for dinner. Impressing them with a delicious meal is one of the nicest things to do.

Cat Deeley

Bagpuss fan Cat was amazed to get an invitation to call her heroine Debbie Harry and has happy memories whenever she sees Van Gogh's Sunflowers

I really loved Bagpuss when I was a little girl. We had him on SM:tv, which I used to present, and it was great because the whole crew had pictures taken with him. He never seems to age, old Bagpuss. He's still yellow and a bit worn round the edges. So sweet!

The Ivy in London's West End is a favourite restaurant of mine because the food is great. The staff are really lovely and there's always a chance of seeing someone famous eating there.

I love kick boxing and I have a personal trainer who comes round and holds up pads that I kick like crazy for an hour. Luckily, I haven't missed and hit her yet. I don't need to picture anyone I hate when I do it because I have so much pent-up energy, which I release.

Breakfast At Tiffany's is my favourite movie because I absolutely adore Audrey Hepburn. It's one of those films you can put on when the weather outside is horrible and you instantly feel warm inside.

I used to have a poster of Van Gogh's Sunflowers on my bedroom wall when I shared a flat with two other girls. Now I'm lucky enough to have my own flat, but whenever I see that painting, it reminds me of the fun we had.

The Godfather by Mario Puzo is brilliant and, although it's extremely long, I went through it really fast. Everyone rightfully hails the Godfather films as being great masterpieces, but the book is totally engrossing as well. Once I started reading, I couldn't put it down.

Meeting one of my all-time heroines, Debbie Harry from Blondie, was amazing. She even gave me her phone number and said: 'Whenever you're in New York, give me a call.' I was totally gobsmacked.

I enjoy visiting the Natural History Museum because it's such a beautiful and fascinating place. When the London Fashion Week shows were held there, I got to know the place really well. So now I go back to check out the incredible exhibits on display.

Vic Reeves

Vic, who was born James Moir in Darlington, loves Tesco, is addicted to snowboarding, collects rare vehicles and enjoys riding on pigs

Ever since the first time I went snowboarding in America, I've been addicted. I even dyed my hair blond like a totally rad dude! I got too cocky at first and tried some jumps. I flew off and hit a wall of ice, bruising myself quite badly.

My all-time comic hero is Eric Morecambe. He had wonderful timing and a face that made you crack up. I have a portrait of him at home – I paint figurative stuff mainly. I once started to do a seascape but gave up. I just can't get that feeling of distance into the picture.

Rare vehicles have always been a passion of mine. I sold my motorbikes because I realised that, as a responsible parent, I shouldn't be bombing around on something that does 160mph. I kept a Royal Enfield Continental GT, although petrol keeps leaking out of it and sparks fly off.

I really like tailor-made suits. I've got some that I ordered from a bloke in Deptford High Street in Southeast London. I have a few from Armani and I even bought a light cream one from Marks & Spencer.

Shopping at Tesco is great – we've got a huge hypermarket in Ashford, Kent, and it sells everything. We go once a week and it takes us about an hour to unload the car. Even my daughter Alice has to help out carrying the Weetabix in.

I'm happier living in Kent than London. I didn't want my children to grow up in an overpopulated, smog-filled environment. We've just moved to a house in Charing. It's very handy for popping into London for meetings – it only takes half an hour.

I love buying antiques. I once bought a grandfather clock that doesn't work. It was great for hiding in when I used to play hide-and-seek with Alice. I had to pretend she wasn't in there when I looked.

I really liked living and working on a rare breed farm because I got to ride around on the backs of my pigs. I talked to them about the meaning of life and scratched their bellies, too. I had two ducks and three rare Dexter cows. I could never kill my pigs and eat them, though – I was too attached to them.

Jayne Middlemiss

Jayne hated Maggie Thatcher, is a fan of the Sex Pistols and worships Alan Shearer

I love Newcastle, even though I don't go home too often these days. A journalist once asked me what I liked about it and I told him we all sit around in Newcastle United shirts singing When The Boat Comes In, eating coal and drinking Newcastle Brown Ale.

I passionately hated everything about Maggie Thatcher as prime minister. She was scary! And she single-handedly destroyed the coal mining industry and so many local communities in the North East. My dad was a miner and he was on strike for ages. He's my hero – he's smart, funny, has a really good musical sense and must have hated his job.

I love alternative medicine and spent a small fortune on cranial osteopathy. It involves the manipulation of bones in your head and helps me to chill out. I first had it after a skiing accident and it costs me about £40 a session, but it's worth it.

I think Van Gogh was a genius, albeit a tragic one. Do you know he's thought to have sold only one painting during his lifetime? My favourite is The Asylum Garden At Arles – the Provençal town in the south of France where he lived and eventually chopped off his ear.

Alan Shearer is a total god where I'm from. He was one of those completely inspirational players and I loved watching him on the pitch.

I treasure my copy of Never Mind The Bollocks by The Sex Pistols. When it came out, my mum wouldn't let me have it because I was only about 10. I used to tell people that it was Johnny Rotten who taught me how to swear.

Brief Encounter is my favourite film. It's full of lines like, 'Oh, I seem to have something in my eye.' It's really posh and I find that kind of thing very funny. It stars Trevor Howard and Celia Johnson. Richard Burton and Sophia Loren made a terrible TV remake of it in 1974.

I like reading books about cats because every breed has a totally individual character. I have a beautiful tortoiseshell cat called Sweets who's typically sweet-natured.

Chris Evans

Chris is passionate about playing golf with his buddies, loves building his collection of luxury cars and gets a thrill from roller coasters

I grew up on 70s television, it's what inspired me. Even now I can sit around for hours on end watching reruns of shows like Tiswas, Blue Peter, Ask Aspel and Swap Shop. People like Noel Edmonds and Michael Aspel are still great.

I never used to like Terry Wogan much on TV, probably because he was on it about three times a week. He's brilliant on the radio, though, a real genius. He's a natural and a lot funnier than people credit him for. If there was one radio show I wouldn't miss, it's his.

I love luxury cars – I've had a Porsche, a Bentley, and a Jeep in the past. But Ferraris are my favourite. As well as looking great, they're a good investment, too. The best is a lovely blue 1972 Ferrari Dino. But I do stand out in mine at times, which can be a hassle.

Blackpool is a wonderful place, which reminds me of my childhood and very happy memories. My dad died when I was only 14 and we had some great times on holiday there together. I used to love the trams, the Pleasure Beach and the seaside. I like going back even now.

Playing golf has been a passion of mine since I was young, when it was probably very unfashionable. I got very good at it as a teenager. It's a great way to unwind with my mates and is definitely not naff.

I love the thrill of roller coasters and the Nemesis ride at Alton Towers is amazing. I was scared out of my wits, but it really gets the heart pumping. I'm only glad I didn't have breakfast beforehand.

A good pillow is one of my few luxuries. I always buy the most expensive duck-down pillows because they look after your back, your head and your mind. I don't know how people can buy £3 pillows. They're really important.

Cher is lust on legs – one of the sexiest women in the world. I'm lucky to be able to say that my most exciting dream of meeting her on my show happened. Then she said she'd never had a ginger-haired man and I nearly died. I was almost speechless.

Claire Sweeney

Claire has a soft spot for Robert Redford and never gets hangovers on her favourite drink of Jack Daniel's and Coke

Moonlight In Vermont by Frank Sinatra is the most sublime song ever. He and Sammy Davis Jnr are both all-time heroes of mine, but Frank was called the Chairman of the Board. His voice will last for ever.

My favourite read is Geri Halliwell's autobiography If Only. It's fascinating how she copes with the pressures of fame.

I bought my first perfume, White Linen by Estée Lauder, when I was 14. I've started using it again. I've tried every other brand in between, but I've gone back to the one I first started with.

The Way We Were is my all-time favourite film. I had my first-ever crush on Robert Redford. Even today I think many women agree that his blue eyes, blond hair and utter charm are a winning combination. Also, Barbra Streisand sang the theme tune. I really wanted to be her when I was growing up.

I have a real passion for cruise ships because I used to work on one as a singer. I've seen the QE2 on the river Mersey next to where I live. It was lovely to watch it sail by with all the horns blowing. Bliss.

When I go clubbing, Jack Daniel's with ice and Diet Coke is perfect. It's got a real kick, gives you a nice feeling and – as long as I don't mix my drinks – I don't suffer hangovers.

I've had voice lessons since I was 14 and love singing Puccini's Madame Butterfly. When I did Stars In Their Eyes, I was sent to singing coach Mary Hammond, who was impressed with my attempts at the opera.

I love West End shows and Blood Brothers is a favourite. Bernie Nolan, who was in Brookside with me, was in it and it was fabulous. It helps that one of Liverpool's own, Willy Russell, wrote it.

I'm absolutely crazy about playing the fruit machines and roulette wheels in Las Vegas. In fact, I love everything about the place – the glitz, the shows, the hotels. It's just the most amazing city plonked right in the middle of the desert.

Stephen Fry

Comedian and author Stephen loves porridge with marshmallow and he'll never forget the record for the longest bout of hiccups

As a child I enjoyed a particular craving for Scott's Porage Oats. My mother recalls that my brother Roger and I would eat mountains of the stuff and I still start each day by eating a healthy bowlful. Nice with marshmallows as it happens.

I love driving around London in my very own black taxi and I actually don't mind being flagged down by punters. I rather enjoy it and, who knows, one day I might get The Knowledge.

When I was a kid, I learned many of the entries in The Guinness Book Of Records off by heart. My favourite was the longest recorded time for hiccups. It was nine years, six months and 17 days and the man who had them tried everything, including getting people to shout 'Boo!' at him. Then he prayed to St Jude – the patron saint of lost causes – and it worked.

The Bonzo Dog Doo-Dah Band are my favourite group. For me they were the Bonzo God Doo-Dah Band. I modelled my voice on lead singer Vivian Stanshall's. He had an old wireless voice.

Whisky sour is my favourite drink. It consists of four to five parts Scotch, one part lemon juice, one teaspoon of sugar syrup and a dash of egg white. It's served with a lemon slice and a cherry. I'm asthmatic, so I pass out if I drink champagne – I prefer red wines and whiskies.

My favourite hang-out is Soho's Groucho Club. It's always teeming with media types who tend to talk a lot of rubbish. I had my 40th birthday at the Edinburgh Groucho and the owners baked me a chocolate cake.

I still think the Blackadder series stands the test of time as one of the funniest TV comedies. Rowan Atkinson is a complete genius and a perfectionist who simply walks off stage if something goes wrong – he won't ad-lib to the audience, but he's not shy at all.

The Godfather is my favourite film. Its brilliance lies in the way it manages to portray such a cruel, wicked Mafia family at work, yet one still feels real affection for a character such as Michael Corleone, played superbly by the wonderful Al Pacino.

Cybill Shepherd

Comedy actress and singer Cybill decided to go into showbiz after she won a Miss Congeniality contest at 16

I love singing and it's one of my dreams to sing in the wonderful opera La Bohème. I once had a boyfriend who said to me: 'Cybill, why must you sing all the time?' I knew immediately the relationship wasn't going to work.

The colour red is delicious. I've always believed in wearing what suits me rather than what's fashionable. Mustard and chartreuse green might be trendy, but they're yucky. Red's a strong, rich colour, but it doesn't translate well to TV. Producers say it looks like a gaping wound. I wear it anyway and feel like I'm smiling inside.

I'm very proud to call myself a feminist. Women such as Gloria Steinem worked incredibly hard for the quality of life that women enjoy today. I appreciate those who made sacrifices and risked ridicule to make my life as good as it is.

There's no place like Memphis, Tennessee, my home town. I have a house there for holidays because it's so different to Los Angeles. The people in Memphis are very friendly. They say good morning and you don't feel you need to whip out a gun to defend yourself like you do in LA.

I once bought a bra from Frederick's of Hollywood that did wonders for my bust. I think it was called the Captivator and it was much, much cheaper than having a boob job. Best of all, I didn't have to have an anaesthetic. My ex-husband was so impressed, he asked my daughter if I'd had silicone implants.

Clint Eastwood's fantastic. I love older men – they're so much more interesting. I'm not saying I haven't robbed the cradle in my time – and thoroughly enjoyed it – but I really prefer a more mature guy who has something to say.

My treadmill is great. Exercise is like a drug for me – the endorphins make me feel truly wonderful. I try to do a good aerobic work-out at least three times a week. Using a treadmill is perfect because that way I can learn my lines while I'm exercising.

Pearls are wonderful. I wear them with everything and they even look good with jeans.

Dannii Minogue

Dannii gets a kick out of visiting New York's gay clubs and says parachuting also gives her a rush

Mardi Gras in Sydney is so spectacular. I love singing at Gay Pride events because gay men are always so appreciative and supportive of my career. They don't just love the Minogue sisters, they want to be us!

Marlon Brando was a special actor. On The Waterfront is a great film and he looks amazing. I was taught acting in New York by Sandra Leigh, who only takes 15 students at a time – and Marlon was once one, too.

I adored Rex Hunt's Fishing Programme on the Discovery Channel for a quick fix of Down Under. It's still being repeated and reminds me just how beautiful that part of the world is, especially when he goes hunting for barracuda off the coral reefs.

I've always been a huge fan of Paul Whitehouse. I love the work he's done with Harry Enfield, but his own programme The Fast Show was even funnier. I loved the warped, off-beat sense of humour, especially the character who kept saying everything's 'brilliant' because it reminds me of the MTV generation.

My favourite alcoholic drink has to be a shot of vodka mixed with either tonic, lime or soda. Sometimes I also like to drink it mixed with the energy drink Red Bull. It's quite a powerful combination and I usually chug one before I go on stage.

I still feel very passionately about the awful plight of the fighting bears of Turkey after making a film about them for Channel 4's Absolutely Animals. Without question, I'm going to continue to give my support.

Parachuting is a hobby because the adrenaline rush is amazing. I don't think my mum is too keen on me doing it, though, and I'm sure my manager wouldn't be too happy if I ended up with a leg in plaster, either.

My favourite place in the whole world has to be New York, a city that truly never sleeps. When I was living there, I met some really extrovert stars, such as the singer RuPaul, because a lot of my friends were heavily involved in that whole fantastic gay New York clubbing scene. It was such great fun.

Damon Albarn

Gorillaz frontman Damon is a keen backgammon player and loved visiting Iceland so much that he bought a flat there

When I was about 12 or 13, the music of Madness meant a lot to me. I even tried to copy their fashion style by turning up at my local youth club dressed like them.

A few years ago, I bought a small flat in Reykjavik in Iceland because I've always liked visiting the place. I decided it was time to have somewhere there to call my own. I love Iceland because it's at the top of the world. I'm also drawn to dark, cold places and it's very, very cold there.

I'm a bit of a backgammon addict. A friend of mine loves playing it, too, and it's added a whole new dimension to our relationship – especially when we try to play after a few drinks. It makes the game a little more interesting!

I used to live very near the Portobello Road and absolutely loved walking around Portobello Market, especially early in the mornings. I still get a lot of my clothes there. I think Notting Hill is one of the best areas to live in London, with all its beautiful early Victorian terraced streets.

If I'm feeling flashy, I love going to a London restaurant called 192, located at 192 Kensington Park Road. I used to live just a short walk away, so it was very handy. It's quite trendy really and always has a few celebrities eating there. I like taking my mum and sister and treating them to lunch or dinner.

The Lord Of The Rings was my favourite book when I was growing up. I also liked the Tolkien posters you could buy. The book is totally magical, what with all those white wizards encountering evil, smelly, big-nosed goblins.

Marvin Gaye's Sexual Healing is just a fabulous piece of music. I love all the old Motown recordings he made before it, too. That was just an incredible period of music making. It must have been amazing to be a part of that whole Detroit scene.

I really fancied Kate Bush when she first started out. When her single Wuthering Heights went to No 1, her face was suddenly plastered everywhere and, as I recall, she looked absolutely amazing.

Barbara Windsor

I love my husband Scott and I don't know what I would have done without him. He's always there for me and very old for his age, with a sensible head on his shoulders. But we have a lot of fun together, too.

I met John Major at a showbiz bash. He's absolutely gorgeous, very intelligent and witty. It's a shame about his grey image because I find him very exciting – and, yes, even a bit sexy.

I have to watch my weight because I'm small. I took slimming pills once – when I had to wear a G-string for the film Carry On Again Doctor. Some quack gave me pills and an injection and I went down from 7 to 6st and also lost four inches off my boobs. Never again!

I'm traditional when it comes to food and I always make an effort with the good old Sunday roast. There aren't many Sundays when I don't cook one. I like to alternate between pork, lamb and beef – with plenty of trimmings, of course.

I love being pampered, but I could never have cosmetic surgery. I've had a face-lift without surgery. They send electrical impulses through the skin to rejuvenate old muscles and stimulate the face. I had it done after seeing what I looked like on EastEnders and I reckon it's made me look and feel much better.

Anna Karen, who played my sister in EastEnders and Olive in On The Buses, has been my best friend since the 60s. She was actually a nightclub stripper when we first met. She's stunning and very bright and we speak on the phone about four times a week.

Prince Edward is a real sweetie. He phoned me personally to ask me to appear in the Royal It's A Knockout. Luckily my agent warned me he might call, so when he rang and said: 'I'm Prince Edward,' I didn't say: 'Yes and I'm the Queen Mum.'

I don't like the term 'toy boy', but younger men seem to have much more energy, which they need to keep up with my lifestyle. I've never thought about age difference. I like men for who they are, not for what age they happen to be.

Jade Goody

BB3 contestant Jade became an unexpected celebrity, famous for her dumb quotes. She loves eating curry and watching her favourite film Top Gun

Ugly by Constance Briscoe is really gripping. It's an autobiography about the abuse the author suffered as a child. It's quite depressing and had me in tears. On a lighter note, I love my Harry Potter books.

When I'm in a naughty mood, I'll always order a curry. I'm not really into spicy curries, so I usually get a lamb balti, keema naan and Bombay potatoes for my perfect takeaway.

Jack Nicholson is mesmerising to watch. He was brilliant in One Flew Over The Cuckoo's Nest and Anger Management. He can turn his hand to so many different characters – and that's what I love about him.

Marilyn Monroe's one of those icons I really admire. She was beautiful, a legend and took chances to better herself. She had a 'live for the moment' attitude that I respect.

I've been playing Chris Brown's album constantly. He's a new R&B artist from America who's really young, cute and talented. I can't believe he's still a teenager – his music is the nuts.

I wet myself every time I see The Simple Life with Paris Hilton and Nicole Richie. It's great hangover TV and the girls make me laugh so much with the stupid things they get up to.

Nothing beats the smell of freshly baked bread when you walk into a bakery. It's delicious and always makes my mouth water.

Puerto Banus in Marbella, Spain, is the best for a girls' holiday. One year, 27 of us went – it was brilliant. Plenty of sun, sea – and fun, of course!

I've watched Top Gun about 35 times – and only saw it for the first time two years ago. Tom Cruise is so gorgeous in it and it's got so much passion.

I had a massive crush on Brian Harvey from East 17 when I was younger and I even camped outside his house once. All he did was walk past me and smile, but I was in love. Some people might reckon the boys look a bit ropey these days, but East 17 were never smooth and pretty like Take That – they were the rough and ready ones.

Alice Cooper

Rock legend Alice gets his inspiration from watching bad kung fu movies and enjoys relaxing at his holiday home in Maui

For a holiday destination, it's hard to beat Maui. I've got a holiday home out there. Hawaii's a great place for playing golf and spending some time by myself to relax.

I'm a horror movie addict and have to see every scary film. I hate boring dramas like Gosford Park, which was the worst film ever. Critics say it's great. Better than Jaws 3-D? Come on, the shark eats a helicopter!

I've collected about 300 watches. They're all shapes and sizes – it doesn't matter what make they are as long as the face is unique. I try to find the oldest, weirdest timepieces. It's the only obsession I have.

Apart from The Beatles and The Stones, I'd say the best band are The Yardbirds. The line-up kept changing, but they were top musicians. Look at the guitar players – Jimmy Page, Jeff Beck and Eric Clapton!

I love to play golf. It's fantastic because you play against yourself and against the course. It's easy to break clubs, that's the whole philosophy behind a lot of pros. They say the best way to hit a ball is to pretend you're throwing your club. I've only been playing since I've lived in LA. Just keep your head down and throw your club at the ball and it'll go further.

My favourite actor is Jimmy Stewart. He was brilliant in old movies such as Harvey and Mr Smith Goes To Washington. He was the bubbly, all-American guy who everyone liked.

Some of my fans would probably have my own worst ever songs, such as I Love The Dead, played at their funeral. If it were up to me, I'd do the opposite and have a hymn played – maybe How Great Thou Art.

Before performing, I watch really bad kung fu movies. I'm not talking Bruce Lee here – I'm talking about really bad ones, like seven vampires versus a load of monks. They're really horrible – I've got thousands of them.

The most romantic city I've ever been to is Budapest. It's got that fantastic 'old world' charm. I could just walk around it all day and never get bored. It's beautiful.

Debbie Harry

Blondie singer Debbie once rolled in the mud at Woodstock and admired Brooke Shields so much she wrote a song about her

I'm a big fan of Brooke Shields – she was great in the TV sitcom Suddenly Susan. I did a photo shoot with her once and she was a sweet person. I'd seen her act brilliantly in a film called Pretty Baby, so I wrote a song – Pretty Baby – about her.

I love Japanese Chin dogs – they have the flat face of a pug. They were forerunners of the King Charles spaniel – so are a very rare old breed.

Rear Window is a terrific Hitchcock thriller and was actually written about my New York apartment building. There are about 4,000 apartments and I can see into about 600 of them. It's a massive place, but has turned into a bit of a yuppie ghetto.

I really admire RuPaul. He's great at presenting his own talk show. I can remember when I first met him. A friend of his tipped him off that I was eating in a New York restaurant and RuPaul turned up with a copy of my latest album, asking me to sign it.

Andy Warhol was a talented person who I was lucky to meet many times. I moved to New York in 1965 and wanted to be a painter, so I enjoyed getting to know such a one-off character. Fortunately, he did a really nice portrait of me in 1980.

Woodstock was an amazing experience. Peace and love was the message and it really was a wonderful event, unlike anything else I've ever been to. I think that I actually got to roll around in some mud, too!

John Waters is a brilliant director and also an old friend of mine. He's got such an imaginative mind and has never been afraid of making B-movies like Hairspray that don't fit in with that whole Hollywood scene.

Naked Lunch by William S Burroughs is one of my favourite books. It's such a creative piece of work that really fires the reader's imagination. William was also a dear friend until he died in 1997.

I love to go to LA to see my friends from New York who have moved there. It's an adventure and is a little more relaxed. The only thing I don't like is the driving.

Denise Van Outen

Former Big Breakfast presenter Denise loves Clinique fake tan and is a fan of Kylie Minogue records

I had a Girl's World – one of those heads on a stand – because I was a very girly little girl. I'd sit and play with it for hours, doing the make-up, playing with the hair and creating different styles. I was totally obsessed with it.

I discovered sushi about 10 years ago and I've never looked back since. I used to eat plain sorts of food, but I'm now a complete sushi convert. It's so light and fresh and I love the way it makes me feel after I've eaten it. If I could describe myself as a certain dish, it would be a sushi Californian roll because it's quite classy, good to look at and has a bit of a kick to it.

I used to spend a fortune on Clinique's spray-on fake tan, especially when I was getting up really early to do The Big Breakfast TV show. I guess I need to find a gym with some decent sunbeds because we all look better with a bit of colour.

The lobster ravioli at Zilli Fish in Soho does it for me every time. Aldo Zilli is definitely my favourite chef because he's a great cook, he makes me laugh and is a nutter, just like myself. A few years ago, I tried oysters and now I find myself craving them.

I'm a huge fan of Alison Steadman, especially in Life Is Sweet and Abigail's Party. She's one of our finest actresses and when I watch these two classic productions, which were directed by her ex-husband Mike Leigh, I can't stop laughing at her characters.

The kind of music I really go for is anything that reminds me of old school disco days. I especially love classic Kylie Minogue records. She's amazing.

Vodka and cranberry juice is my favourite tipple on a night out with the girls. I don't really have a preference for which brand of vodka it is, but I do like plenty of ice to keep my drink cool.

I love using my Louis Vuitton bag, although it wasn't cheap. I really don't think there's any point in spending huge amounts on things that aren't made really well. Hopefully, it'll last me for years and years.

Trevor McDonald

Trevor unwinds by listening to slushy love songs, adores Barbados and enjoys cricket

I'm a huge Beethoven fan. I love his Ninth Symphony and his Emperor Concerto, but my all-time favourite is the Violin Concerto. I like to think that when you die, the first sound you hear – the one that confirms for you that you're in heaven – would be Beethoven's Violin Concerto.

My love of cricket developed in the womb, I think – it's like a West Indian contagion. I remember in Trinidad playing from the age of four, hammering in stumps in neighbours' back yards and fashioning bats from the branches of coconut trees. It was absolutely fantastic. All of the islands were wrapped up in it.

I enjoy listening to love songs. One of my favourites is Ocean Drive by the Lighthouse Family. I'm a bit of a softie, really. It's nice to unwind to songs like that after hearing all the horror stories you have to deal with as a journalist.

I prefer to spend my winters in Barbados. It's great to be away from the cold of Britain and get into the heat of the Caribbean. I can sit under a palm tree, smoke a cigar, read a book and have people bring me rum punches whenever I need them.

The Guns Of Navarone is the greatest film of all time. It's filled with heroic deeds of the kind I couldn't possibly contemplate myself, but I love to watch others risking everything for what they believe in.

Jamie Lee Curtis is my favourite film star. I thought she was terrific in True Lies. They teased me at work because I was raving so much about Jamie the day after I first saw that film.

I read all the time and my favourite book changes from year to year. But the one I like rereading most is The Fatal Shore by Robert Hughes. He lives in New York and is a great art critic and historian. The book's about the emigration of people from Georgian England and the making of Australia.

I can't get enough of TV comedies. David Jason is just magnificent in Only Fools And Horses. Any episode of that would come pretty high up on my list of all-time favourite television moments.

Donna Summer

Donna enjoys eating chicken with couscous, loves to ride horses and has an unusual hobby of collecting antique chairs

Under The Tuscan Sun is a great movie. I like the idea of just being frivolous and doing what you want to do. I've seen it several times, but I'm too embarrassed to keep asking my husband if I can watch it again.

Marvin Gaye is an inspiration to my career. His classic What's Going On was a real human cry, but musical and sensual at the same time. People relate to it even now that he's dead.

I love chicken with couscous. You can eat it with your fingers or with a spoon. It's very communal because everyone eats from the same dish. It's really interesting food.

The US sitcom My Wife And Kids always has me in fits of laughter. My daughter Brooklyn starred in the show. Her character was pregnant and, when I went on set to watch, she had a prosthetic bump which was so lifelike it blew my mind.

Tiger Woods is brilliant – he's one of my favourite sportsmen. He breathed new life into golf and brought it to the attention of a new generation. It's a sport that everyone can play and his swing changed everyone's perceptions of the game.

I love collecting chairs. I've found some that are so strange, I don't know how they were used. I'm a big fan of antique chairs – I love coming to the UK and finding treasures.

I absolutely adore Marrakech. I was privileged to be a guest of the King of Morocco and I spent an amazing week there. It gave me such a great connection with the past. I can't wait to go back.

I read the Bible more than any other book. My grandfather was a minister and I've read it pretty much cover to cover. Is there a better book? It's juicy with lots of love stories.

Horses are my favourite animals. I used to ride a lot – I'll start again when my career slows down. I love talking to horses. They're so intelligent and beautiful.

Ralph Lauren Blue is a gorgeous perfume. It's really pleasant and not too heavy. I like wearing a scent that people don't immediately recognise.

Goldie Hawn

Goldie loves afternoon tea, Sarah Ferguson and Mick Jagger, living in Vancouver and Valentine's Day with partner Kurt Russell

A favourite film of mine has to be Stanley Kubrick's A Clockwork Orange. It's incredible. There was a lot of what he called 'the old in and out' in that movie and I know that for many years he banned the film from being screened in the UK.

These days I live in Vancouver, Canada, and it really is a beautiful city. It makes a nice change from Los Angeles and it's so clean – you can actually breathe in fresh air all day long. I love the countryside and Vancouver has a real link with nature.

One of the perks of being a movie star is meeting your musical heroes. I've been lucky enough to meet Mick Jagger several times. It's wonderful because I'm a huge Rolling Stones fan.

I love the traditions of British life. I really enjoyed having afternoon tea at The Dorchester hotel in London's Park Lane. You guys are so civilised.

I think Peter Sellers was a genius. I acted with him in the movie There's A Girl In My Soup way back in 1970 and I always laugh when I remember how clever he was and how he made us all fall about the place. I was recently asked to recount all the stories I have of Peter and I just kept thinking what a wonderful time it was working with him.

I love modern poetry – you know, the beatnik generation. Some of Jim Morrison's writing was really cool, too. I thought he looked pretty nice – in fact, I liked his looks a lot. His drug problem would have turned me off a bit, though.

I have always thought that Valentine's Day is a very special day. Kurt and I first got together in 1983 and I think people who live together forget to charm each other. The passion dies and your sexuality goes up and down – so it's a lovely opportunity to try to charm each other again, even if it's just for one day.

Sarah Ferguson really makes me laugh and I think Americans love her television commercials in particular. I heard that she once said she wanted a relationship with the Duke of York similar to mine with Kurt. She's so funny!

Donny Osmond

Daredevil Donny loves motor racing and wants to drive in the Le Mans race and bungee jump off a bridge

If I could eat anything in the world, it'd be fresh, green peas from my home state of Utah. They're so delicious. You shouldn't even put salt or butter on them – just pop them out of their shell and eat.

Standing For Something by Gordon B Hinckley is the best book I've ever read. It deals brilliantly with the practicalities of living and just being kind to fellow human beings.

The Score is one of the best films I've seen. It's got an all-star cast, with Ed Norton, Marlon Brando and Robert De Niro, who's my all-time favourite actor. I doubt if you'll see three such great male actors cast in the same movie ever again.

My favourite holiday destination has always been Hawaii and, in particular, the paradise resort of Kauai. I've been going to Hawaii for years, ever since my sister Marie and I made a movie there in 1978.

My favourite building has to be the Salt Lake Temple in Utah, where my wife Debbie and I got married in 1978. It isn't just for sentimental reasons – I think it's also a really beautiful place to sit and reflect.

A classic black Armani suit is truly an object of great beauty. Every time I visit Italy, where one of my sons lives, I go clothes shopping.

My latest passion is bungee jumping. I once jumped off some scaffolding in Vancouver. I'd love to jump off a bridge or a tall building one day. Reverse bungee jumping is even more of a thrill.

Stevie Wonder's Songs In The Key Of Life is definitely the finest pop album I've ever heard. I'd recommend anyone who wants to be a songwriter to listen to songs such as Sir Duke and Isn't She Lovely and learn from the great man.

I love motor racing because I'm a daredevil at heart. I actually won a race in 1991 against other professionals, driving a Lotus at speeds of up to 130mph. Driving in the Le Mans 24-hour race would be my ultimate dream, but I'm not quite ready for that kind of challenge yet.

Jennifer Ellison

Jennifer never tires of watching Pretty Woman, is a fan of The Commodores and could have been a ballerina

Mauritius looks so peaceful and beautiful. Some friends I know have been there and they say it's just the most perfect place to get away to if you're having a really hectic time. I might end up loving it so much that I'd never come back.

Julia Roberts is brilliant in Pretty Woman and I always find myself watching this film every couple of years or so. She's been such a wonderful actress for years and really deserved her Oscar for her portrayal of Erin Brockovich.

I spend a fortune on the BeneFit cosmetics range, which you can now get from larger branches of Boots. I love MAC products, too, but BeneFit stuff is considerably cheaper and the quality is still as good.

Ballet has been my biggest passion ever since I started attending dance classes at the age of three. I decided to stop when I was 15 because it involved four hours of practice a day. In the end, I didn't want to spend all my spare time doing it – but not before I had danced at the Royal Ballet School in London.

Easy, written by Lionel Richie and performed by The Commodores, is my favourite song of all time. It brings back many childhood memories and is a really great chilled-out tune. It never sounds better than when it's played on a Sunday morning while you're getting over a hangover.

I loved the old Budweiser adverts – they were absolutely hilarious. I went through a stage of getting about 10 text messages a day on my mobile phone from friends just saying 'Whassup?', which at the time was really funny.

Ralph Lauren Romance is my favourite perfume. It comes in a beautiful, tiny, square bottle and has a lovely fruity smell that's great for both day and night. I always get comments about it. I got my first bottle from my mum for my 15th birthday.

I'm a member of the Total Fitness health clubs. I don't go half as often as I should, so it's been a bit of a waste of money. I do like the machines they've got and the staff are very helpful.

Hannah Waterman

Perth in Western Australia is the most beautiful place I've ever visited. I went with my dad Dennis quite a few times when I was a child. Then, when I was 16, I returned for four weeks and had the holiday of a lifetime. I spent most of my time on the beach just preparing for the trauma of A level exams upon my return to the UK.

I have a bit of a thing for Russell Crowe. After seeing him in Gladiator, I just thought: 'That man is a god!' Very superficial of me, I know.

Absolut Vodka is my favourite drink. I love working my way through the different flavours during an evening – with a dash of lemonade, of course. There are so many different flavours that it gives every drink a fresh new taste.

My mum lives in Devon and recently I was fortunate enough to eat at Rick Stein's seafood restaurant in nearby Padstow, Cornwall. The restaurant is right on the harbour and I ate lots of wonderful oysters, crabs and mussels. That has to be my favourite food.

Virginia Woolf's To The Lighthouse is my favourite book. It reminds me of a wonderful English teacher who taught me at A level. I even did my university interview on the book, so I usually manage to sound quite an authority.

While My Guitar Gently Weeps on The Beatles' 'White Album' has to be the greatest song ever written. It's a George Harrison composition and his songs were always really underrated. This is my dad's influence – he was always playing The Beatles, Bob Dylan and Eric Clapton songs.

Paul Smith is definitely my favourite designer – he tailors so superbly for women. He's a craftsman who's really worth the money. I've got more of his clothes than any other designer's.

I've started wearing a new Jean Paul Gaultier perfume called Fragile, which comes in a snowstorm shaker. I'm also a big fan of Allure by Chanel, so now I'm torn between the two and can't decide which is my favourite.

Daniel Bedingfield

Daniel loves reading comic books and wants to own a Canadian pet squirrel

The most beautiful and relaxing place in the world is Auckland in New Zealand. Oh, and I was born there, so obviously I love it.

I wish I could have met Frank Sinatra. He put so much emotion into his voice with so much variation in its tone. He could take your heart and wring it out. My Way and Theme From New York, New York are absolute classics.

I'm always playing Revolver by The Beatles. They were pioneers – they took obscure sounds from all over the place and made them popular. Every song sounds fresh. The Beatles had a huge influence on 80s and 90s music.

I'm a big South Africa fan when it comes to cricket. I think Jonty Rhodes is an absolute god in the game and was a great fielder.

I got my love of Thai food from my mum, who travelled a lot when she was younger. My favourite recipe is tom ka kai, which contains mushrooms, chicken and coconut milk.

My favourite book ever is Ender's Game by Orson Scott Card. It's about an invasion of the earth by aliens and the kids who save the planet.

I'm passionate about the movie The Last Of The Mohicans. This is mainly because the colours are intense and it's not at all cheesy. It's powerful and brutal. There's lots of action and it's a good, honest film.

My favourite comic books are the Out There series by the Cliffhanger crew. I am a big fan of the comics because of the artwork in them. Whenever I get some spare time, I just sit in and read my backlog.

Natalie Portman is the most attractive woman in the universe. I never miss any of her films. From her early appearance as a young girl in the thriller Leon to her recent role in the Stars Wars prequels, she's been exceptional.

I've always wanted a pet squirrel. A grey one would do, but the black ones they have in Canada are so beautiful. I don't think it's legal to keep them as pets, though, is it?

Charlie Brooks

Charlie Brooks would love a massage chair, is inspired by Marilyn Monroe and wants Brad Pitt for his mind

My favourite film of the 90s was Leaving Las Vegas. Nicolas Cage has never been better, playing a down-and-out drunk, and Elizabeth Shue was incredible as the prostitute who comforts him.

My favourite restaurant is a little Thai place called Burlington Café in Chiswick, West London. The people who work there are a bit abrupt, but they don't mind you having a good time, too. Funny place!

Marilyn Monroe is my inspiration – especially the way she looks in Some Like It Hot. She was so beautiful and so womanly. Back in those days, there was no pressure on actresses or models to be skinny or to conform to the impossible supermodel shape of today.

Lovelife by a group called Lush is my favourite album. The lyrics remind me of growing up. The words made so much sense to me at 14. I'm not sure the group are even still together, though.

Lake Tahoe in California is the most amazing looking place in the world. It's a skiing resort – I once went for Christmas and New Year and the snow was knee high. I want to go back there more than anywhere else in the world.

I know it's not a very original choice, but Men Are From Mars, Women Are From Venus is the book that I would go back and read again if I had the time. I think I will probably take it with me on my next holiday.

I want someone to buy me one of those electric massage chairs. They look amazing and my idea of heaven is to have a permanent massage with hands tingling my back.

Jack Dee is the funniest man on TV. He has me in stitches with his dry humour. His one-liners are hilarious and he's quite good looking in a strange kind of way.

I love Brad Pitt – but for his beautiful mind, not his body. The mind is always the most important thing for me. He did look pretty fit in the film Fight Club, though. I would definitely snog him.

86

Jerry Hall

Model and actress Jerry loves tuberose flowers, horse riding, eating barbecue crisps and watching the classic Mae West film Goin' To Town

My favourite book has to be Wide Sargasso Sea by Jean Rhys. I reread it as part of an Open University course. It's a clever prequel to Charlotte Brontë's Jane Eyre.

I've always loved horses. I have a horse farm and my daughters Georgia May and Elizabeth also keep horses. I'm a pretty good rider. I don't like to do anything too dangerous, but I love gentle riding.

I'm hooked on barbecue crisps. Contrary to what you may think about models, I eat a lot, but I just don't gain weight. I need to keep my energy levels up or I droop.

I go for long walks and do sit-ups to keep in shape. Plus, I don't eat any sugar, so that helps.

The most memorable place I've been to is the Rialto Bridge in Venice. I went there on holiday and have amazing memories of looking down the famous Grand Canal.

Tuberose is my favourite flower of all. It smells really amazing – the fragrance just fills the whole room – and it reminds me of the beautiful island of Bali, where it grows.

Nina Simone's Blue For You is a special song for me. I love her voice. I've been listening to her songs for years and years and I just never get tired of them. I love Billie Holiday and French singer Edith Piaf, too. I must admit I love torch singers. I guess it's all the drama they evoke.

My favourite perfume is Fracas by Robert Piguet. I've been wearing it since I was 18 and I love it because it smells just like fresh flowers.

I love ballet and my favourite dancer is Sylvie Guillem. She's divine – I think she's the greatest dancer. It's one thing to possess the technical know-how, but another to have her incredible drama and star appeal. She's unbelievable – watching her gives me goosebumps.

Mae West's Goin' To Town is my favourite film and I never get tired of it. My children love it, too, and we watch it all the time. Mae West is one of my heroines. I love her classic comic one-liners.

Gary Lineker

Gary loves watching The Simpsons, wishes he could play golf like Tiger Woods and enjoys a nice glass of red wine

I like a drop of claret. It helps me sleep and I've also heard that a glass of red wine now and then is good for you. But, to be honest, I drink it simply because I really enjoy it.

The Simpsons is great TV. It appeals to children and is also interesting enough to adults. It's both good fun and very clever.

Wembley Stadium was a bit of a dump, so I'm not sorry they knocked it down. But it holds wonderful memories. Winning the FA Cup there with Spurs in 1991 was one of the great moments of my life.

I found the film Schindler's List totally unforgettable. It made pretty depressing viewing, but it was very moving.

I had three great years living in Barcelona. It's one of those places that has everything – brilliant climate, close to the coast, mountains nearby, great architecture, excellent restaurants and superb nightlife.

When I was growing up, I used to watch Pele on TV. He was the greatest footballer of all time. The first time I saw him was when he played against England in the 1970 World Cup. When I was living in Japan, he rang me out of the blue and asked if I fancied going out for a drink. I was shaking at the thought of meeting him.

Nick Hornby's book Fever Pitch is a big favourite of mine. I really identified with the way his love of football was part of everything in his life, including his relationships with women. The film was nowhere near as good as the book, though.

Tiger Woods is awesome at what he does. He's just so much better than anyone else around. I've been playing golf since I was young, but only really got into it since I stopped playing football professionally.

I love the adverts I've done for Walkers Crisps. My favourite was the one we made with Gazza crying. When they put the contraption on his face that made the tears start flowing, we both fell about laughing. It was at least two hours before either of us could keep a straight face long enough to film the advert.

Joanna Lumley

Actress Joanna adores ballet dancing, loves to paint and thinks London is a really fantastic place to live

I've met Muhammad Ali twice. I adore sportsmen. I think there's something overwhelming about someone who has been supreme at their sport. He was charming and flawless to watch.

Of all the world's cities, London is the one I like best. I know it inside out and not at all. I adopted it when I first came to stay at the age of 18 or 19 when I was modelling and I love living here. When I see tourists taking pictures of Big Ben, I think: 'You're so lucky, you're going to adore it here.'

I was born in India and have always loved mountains, but particularly the Himalayas. It is the most colossal mountain range. It puts life into perspective.

I have a wonderful holiday home in Scotland. It was derelict when I first saw it, but is set among hills in Dumfriesshire. There's a wonderful feeling of emptiness and distance, with buzzards and curlews flying overhead.

I've always adored classical music. Beethoven is my favourite composer and has been since I was about seven. His music is enormously comforting at times and rousing at others. I also confess to a weakness for Elvis Presley – I'd have queued for days, knee deep in water, to see him.

I am very keen on the work of the charity Compassion For Animals. I've been a vegetarian for a long time. It was a moral decision because I realised I could live without anything having to die for me.

I love to paint and draw, but wouldn't dream of exhibiting. I love going to galleries. Tiepolo is my favourite artist. He was Italian and worked on vast frescoes, ceilings and murals in palaces and churches. His faces don't look old-fashioned – they could be you or me today.

I adored ballet dancing when I was young and Dame Margot Fonteyn was a goddess. I remember walking through Covent Garden when I was a teenager and seeing what I thought was a 17-year-old girl walking quite quickly ahead of me. It was only when she turned that I saw her face and realised it was Dame Margot Fonteyn aged 50-something.

Jordan

Jordan – aka Katie Price – is a fan of matching luggage, is crazy about horses and has a fridge full of pitta bread

I love Ibiza so much that I've visited the island three times in one year. I think the nightlife's the best in Europe, but when I stayed in San Antonio with all the lager louts, it got a bit lairy. The best bit was seeing the sunset at Café del Mar.

I really like the look of a CLK Mercedes convertible in navy blue or black. I love to get the top down on a car whenever I can, even in the middle of winter.

One of my favourite pieces of music is a slushy love song called From The Heart by Another Level. I once dated Dane Bowers, who was in the band, and we'd sing it together as a duet.

I love the Jean Paul Gaultier eau de toilette, which comes in a bottle rumoured to be based on Madonna's figure. It smells wonderful and I always keep the bottle afterwards.

I'm a big fan of Manchester United and Teddy Sheringham, who used to play for them. I went crazy when he scored a late equalising goal against Bayern Munich in the 1999 European Champions League Final. I had a brief encounter with Teddy, but it wasn't to be.

I always carry around The Book Of Birthdays by Russell Grant. I love finding out whether people are like their birth-date characteristics. I'm a typical Gemini, born on 22 May, who's described as a 'flirtatious flitter who attracts lovers like ants through a strawberry jam sandwich'.

I'm so addicted to pitta bread that my fridge is jam-packed with it. My gym instructor tells me that it's really good for you. I love eating it dipped into either hummus or taramasalata.

I've spent nearly £1,000 on my Louis Vuitton bags. I think they're incredibly stylish and I bought the personal organiser and a really cute duffel bag to go with them, which I take with me when I go on my hols.

I enjoy horse riding. At 15, Mum bought me an ex-racehorse called Star. He cost a fortune at the vet's, but I adored him. Riding's still a passion.

Ioan Gruffudd

Actor Ioan loves expensive Italian suits, enjoys art exhibitions at the Tate Modern and is very proud to be a Welshman

I was always a huge Morecambe and Wise fan. When I was asked to be a guest performer in The Play What I Wrote, the West End stage show of their lives, I absolutely jumped at the chance. It was a tremendous honour.

Being a very proud Welshman, I have a deep passion for rugby union. Many of the greatest players ever have come from Wales. Although I live in London nowadays, I feel a real tingle of pride whenever I pass the London Welsh RFC ground.

I love Last Resort, which is a really enjoyable low-budget film. It stars Paddy Considine as an amusement arcade owner who falls for a Russian immigrant who's moved to Britain with her young son. It's a really beautiful movie.

I do love wearing a good suit – especially a nice made-to-measure Ozwald Boateng suit or something by Prada. You can't go far wrong with a good-quality Italian suit worn with Italian shoes.

I really enjoy reading Tony Parsons' writing. Playing the lead role in the BBC's Man And Boy alongside the wonderful Natasha Little as my character's wife – who has the good sense to leave me – was great. Tony sums up perfectly how a lot of men feel about relationships.

The Tate Modern is a wonderful example of how to turn an old, disused building into the most stunning of modern art galleries. I'm a big admirer of anything by the artists Matisse and Picasso, so the Tate Modern's exhibition of these two 20th-century greats was well worth a look.

I'm a bit of an Eminem fan. I think The Marshall Mathers LP will be remembered in years to come as a great album. His lyrics are brilliant.

Los Angeles is a great city. I'm living a very suburban, domesticated lifestyle – it's lovely. I find driving easy, but the people who live in LA aren't great drivers.

It's nice to go back to Wales. It can be such a busy lifestyle being an actor and promoting a film, so it's nice to go back home from time to time and have a proper rest.

Julie Walters

Julie has faith in her horoscopes, hates exercise but loves yoga and says visiting Ethiopia with Comic Relief changed her life forever

Exercise is something I can't stand normally, but yoga I think I can handle. My husband Grant introduced me to it and what I like about it is that it involves the minimum of effort, yet you feel stretched and very calm afterwards.

I'm surrounded by animals in our wonderful farm in Sussex. It's great not hearing traffic all the time or pneumatic drills. We had some Vietnamese pot-bellied pigs once, but they wouldn't eat. We bought them a Chinese takeaway to make them feel more at home.

My mother was a very intense Irish woman who once told me I would be in the gutter before I was 20. She pushed her children to do well and never actually said she was proud of me. But after she died, I found a huge stack of cuttings about me. God bless her.

I'm a Pisces and always read my horoscope. I'm quite open-minded about that sort of thing. There's much more out there than scientists would have us believe. I think our future's mapped out for us to some extent.

I always wanted a bigger family, but my daughter Maisie more than makes up for not having more. She fought leukaemia as a little girl, but now she's fine.

Visiting Ethiopia for Comic Relief in 1997 changed my life. It's been struck by civil war, famine and drought, but the people are really beautiful, especially the children. They've got so little but appreciate life. Many are orphans, but they all help each other. My memories of them will live with me forever.

I've played Robert Lindsay's mother, wife and lover in three TV series – so I've got to know him quite well. I suppose you could call us best friends. He always plays little jokes on me when we're acting together, like dropping his trousers in a scene when he's not supposed to.

Spiders absolutely terrify me. I went to see the film Arachnophobia to confront my fear, but it didn't work – I was nearly sick with fright. Whenever a spider finds its way into the room, Maisie and I both scream 'Help!', so I reckon it must be genetic.

Katie Melua

Pulp Fiction is one of the most amazing films I have ever seen. It's so incredibly stylish, clever and funny. I'm a big fan of quirky movies. American Beauty is another favourite.

I've become engrossed in 24 with Kiefer Sutherland on Sky One. I love watching thrillers on TV – once I'd seen the first episode of 24, I was completely hooked.

I could read Iris Murdoch's novel The Sea, The Sea over and over again. It's about a man who moves to a remote cottage on the coast where he's reunited with his childhood sweetheart. I grew up by the sea so I can totally relate to the descriptions of the ocean in the book.

The perfect gift I could be given would be a Fender electric guitar. I have two Spanish guitars and an old electric guitar. My neighbours complain about the noise!

I'm an absolute sucker for any body lotions containing coconut, which is easily the most beautiful fragrance in the world. My real favourite is The Body Shop's Coconut Body Butter, particularly because it isn't tested on animals.

I can lose myself in vintage clothes shops. I love rummaging for one-offs. My best bargain was a deep red coat in Oxfam for just £12 – you'd never know it was second-hand.

My perfect place to get away is Brighton. I adore wrapping up on a winter's day, going to the beach and watching the waves.

Queen's Bohemian Rhapsody is a beautiful song. It reminds me of when I was seven or eight, dancing around our living room in Georgia, Russia, with my family.

My favourite comfort food is hatchapuri, a Georgian dish of fried bread with cheese. My mum has to cook it for me, though – I'm a pretty useless cook unless it's something that I can microwave.

I've met the Queen. She told me she was a fan. No, really! I met her and she explained that she'd heard me singing on the radio and loved my voice. I was amazed.

Jack Osbourne

Jack is an adrenaline junkie who loves his sushi, watches the TV show 24 and thinks that Johnny Depp is an awesome actor

Sushi is my favourite food. I love sushi made with oily tuna and shrimp tempura rolls. Nothing beats a plate of sushi. I think I'm addicted to the stuff.

Australia's a great country – really vibrant. It's super-clean and the people are nice. Thailand and France are cool places, too.

I've seen Saving Private Ryan about 60 times. It's awesome – a great war film. It's really gory, which makes it so good. People's heads get blown off and it looks so believable.

Johnny Got His Gun is an intense book. It's about a soldier from World War 1 who has no arms or legs and is blind, deaf and dumb. It's still banned in US military libraries.

Johnny Depp's an awesome actor – I don't think he's ever done a bad film. Secret Window was a little shitty, but it's Johnny so you have to forgive him. Edward Scissorhands is probably his best. It's a brilliant film.

I'm really into 24. I can't wait for the episode each week, so I buy the box sets and just watch it back-to-back. The storylines are great and Kiefer Sutherland's a fantastic actor.

I think the Houses of Parliament is probably one of the most amazing looking buildings on the planet. You look at the amount of detail – there's just no other building that looks like it. It's very scary-looking, too. It looks like there's some evil emperor who lives in there. Actually there is, his name's Tony Blair.

I love the outdoors and living in a tent – I'm not afraid to rough it. I'm fanatical about climbing. I do these really dangerous things and I'm ready to face each one like a challenge.

Women always tell me I smell like clean laundry, which I think is a good thing. My cologne is Mont Blanc – it usually works wonders for pulling the girls.

I'm mildly superstitious. I've become fanatical about rock climbing and always have to wear my own harness – I won't use anyone else's. I also carry Tibetan prayer beads on every climb. I don't think I could do without them.

Kelly Clarkson

Kelly is a huge fan of Annie Lennox, enjoys watching Friends on TV and likes the sound of Texan rainstorms

I'm a huge fan of Annie Lennox. I think she's the epitome of what a singer should be. She's technically awesome and so passionate and confident with her voice.

Volleyball was my sport at school. I was no good at basketball or soccer, but I could hold my own in volleyball. I quit when I was a senior in order to concentrate on my music.

I'm from Texas and I miss it when I'm away. I love the smell, the sounds, the weather, just everything. We have amazing storms and I've got a rainstorms album on my iPod. I listen to it when I go to bed – it makes me feel at home.

I'm reading three books at the moment. I'm on the fourth Harry Potter and I'm also reading When Godly People Do Ungodly Things by Beth Moore and Ishmael by Daniel Quinn. I wake up a lot at night, so I usually read then.

I love bloody films such as Braveheart and Gladiator. The characters are so strong and emotional. I loved Mel Gibson's character in Braveheart. If you look beyond all the blood and gore, they're really passionate films.

My mum encouraged me to write a diary. I've kept it since I was 10 years old and I find it very therapeutic. Writing songs also helps because not only are you getting the words out, you can also express a mood through the music.

Friends is still the best TV show ever. I could watch it all day and I love Chandler. I ran into one of the cast once, but they weren't very nice at all. It wasn't Matthew Perry, but I got totally blown off.

For my first two years on the road, I had a problem sleeping. I went to a sleep clinic and they suggested vanilla candles. Now I make sure I have them with me whenever I'm away on tour.

White tigers are the most mysterious, strong, beautiful animals I have ever seen. I used to work at Fort Worth Zoo in Texas and you would always find me hanging out at their enclosure.

Michael Bolton

Singer Michael loves Italy, is a fan of the New York Yankees baseball team and enjoys the music of Marvin Gaye

I only met Princess Diana once, at a charity evening. She was an extremely charismatic woman and I would have loved to have known her. I really empathised with her position. She was under such close scrutiny for most of her adult life and the pressure must have been intolerable.

Italy is my favourite country. I think Florence is beautiful and tranquil and I love to escape into the lush countryside of Tuscany. Italian food and wine is wonderful, too – it's a great skill to take simple, fresh ingredients and make a fabulous dish.

Marvin Gaye's music is the best. He had the range, the passion, the soulful approach and the intensity when he wanted to use it. He's my all-time favourite, though Otis Redding comes a very close second.

I prefer my hair cut short now. I had that long style for 30 years. It was restyled by Chris McMillan, who cuts Tom Cruise's hair. The first thing he did was snip off my ponytail and I let out a primal scream. The next morning, I looked in the mirror and felt I'd made the right decision.

My father took me to my first baseball game. I follow the New York Yankees and get to a game whenever I can. Joe Di Maggio is my all-time favourite player.

The most magical moment of my career was when I had my first No I record in America with How Am I Supposed To Live Without You? It took me 20 years to have a hit and even longer to feel secure about my music.

My two Grammy awards mean so much to me. I won the first for Best Male Vocalist in 1990. When it was announced, it was like a dream and everything seemed to be happening in slow motion.

Pavarotti is staggeringly awesome. I love classical opera and I've learned to sing a range of arias. I particularly like Puccini and I'd like to release Nessun Dorma on an album.

I love tennis and practise whenever I can. I've had the opportunity of playing with Pete Sampras, Andre Agassi and Jim Courier at fundraising events.

Kylie Minogue

Kylie loves being dressed by John Galliano, admires actor Willem Dafoe and enjoys a typical Aussie barbecue

I love London. I always look forward to the moment when I get into a London cab and see a red double-decker bus go by.

My favourite song to dance to is probably Whip It by the band Devo. They were the world's first and last new wave, avant-garde, pop terror group. It was a hit in the early 80s – a genius track. When do you ever hear the phrase 'whip it' these days?

Willem Dafoe is such an intense actor. I really admire the way he combines his film career with his passion for the theatre. He's been part of an avant-garde New York theatre group for more than 20 years.

Beck is God – he's the one musician out there I'd most like to work with. I'd even consider making a film with him, as long as I could wear a cowboy hat as well.

John Galliano is an absolute genius. A few years ago he designed all the costumes for one of my tours and he came up with a G-string, a frilly bra and fishnet stockings that were totally outrageous. But it so perfectly reflected what I was thinking at the time, it was frightening.

I'm a huge fan of barbecued seafood, especially in Australia. The fish look amazing before they're even cooked. You can't beat eating mussels marinated in white wine while sitting in the sunshine.

My favourite film has to be Some Like It Hot. It features what is probably Marilyn Monroe's finest screen performance, while Tony Curtis and Jack Lemmon – dressed as women – are simply hilarious.

I admire The Fatal Shore by the Aussie author Robert Hughes. It's 680 pages long and as heavy as a brick, but I kept picking it up and struggling with it until I finished it. It's about the brutal transportation of people to the truly terrifying penal system in Australia before 1850.

Acting is always on the agenda. I've been sidetracked doing singing for a long time, but I'd like to do more acting again. To have a teeny, teeny little part in Moulin Rouge brought it back to the forefront.

Tom Jones

Tom likes champagne and cigars, prefers his underwear to come from Marks & Spencer and is a fan of The Simpsons

Prince is an absolute genius. You can really feel the passion he has for his craft, especially if you're lucky enough to catch one of his late-night private performances when he really lets himself go.

I love the film Red River starring John Wayne and Montgomery Clift. It's a 1948 epic with Wayne in a role that saw him stripped of his characteristic heroic traits. It's wonderful because the actor became something of a caricature of himself soon afterwards.

My favourite tipple has to be Dom Perignon, which is a Moët & Chandon champagne that first appeared in 1921. OK, it's very expensive, but you have to remember that only the finest grapes are used.

I've always been a big fan of The Simpsons. I was flattered when I was asked to be in the show as a cartoon character. I'm definitely an admirer of Marge Simpson – because it was her character who was the closet Tom Jones fan that persuaded her boss to play my song What's New, Pussycat? over the company Tannoy.

There's nothing better than standing at a bar and enjoying a fine Monte Cristo cigar from the Dominican Republic in the Caribbean. I love their salty character and they leave such a wonderful woody flavour on your palate afterwards.

I always wear Marks & Spencer underwear – you can't go wrong. As for the women's knickers that get thrown my way, the British ones are always laundered. But my message to women now is: 'Come to my shows, but keep your knickers on, please.'

There are some excellent vocal groups about now. I particularly like The Backstreet Boys, who have reformed. I think they harmonise well and have recorded some fine songs. I like to know where the current trends are going.

Wuthering Heights is such a wonderful book, with all that passion and dramatic wind and rain on the moors. The whole thing is tremendous. I also love the 1939 film version starring Laurence Olivier and Merle Oberon.

Britt Ekland

Britt can't resist a Starbucks decaff cappuccino, loves to weed the garden and wants to dance with Sir Bob Geldof

I miss the Ford Explorer truck I had in California. The Americans are obsessed with big cars and I loved driving it, but since I've been back in London, I cycle everywhere. I'll probably buy a Mini at some point.

I love nothing better than putting on a pair of old gardening gloves and weeding my garden. It's only small and I have a full-time gardener, but I enjoy it. I never get on my knees or I'd end up with a stiff back and a rather expensive visit to my osteopath.

My first love is an evening at the theatre, especially if I'm going with a group of friends to see something starring my dear friend Stephanie Beacham. She's one of the finest actresses in the world and she's also very beautiful.

Going to a really good restaurant is an essential part of a perfect evening out. One of my favourite haunts is an intimate little Italian restaurant called Il Convivio in London's Belgravia. Finding the perfect restaurant with the right ambience can be tricky, but this place has it.

My favourite drink is probably a Starbucks decaffeinated cappuccino. When I lived in West Hollywood, I could always be found sipping one in the local branch. I'm really glad that, since moving back to London, the chain seems to have followed me here.

My favourite nightclub is The Roxy in Los Angeles. I've had some great nights there over the years and I've seen lots of famous bands play.

Bob Geldof would be my ideal dancing partner. He's very intelligent, attractive and he's done so much good for others.

I hate all the Austin Powers movies with an absolute passion. It really aggravates me because it makes a mockery of England and the 60s. It was a wonderfully creative time when all kinds of artistic people flourished. It was so much more than just 'groovy baby', and I think Liz Hurley looked pretty ridiculous, more 70s than 60s.

I'm passionately anti-smoking. It should be banned in all public places.

Leslie Ash

Leslie loves her tropical banana plant, relaxes on holiday in Barbados and shops via the internet

I read Bridget Jones's Diary on holiday in Barbados and laughed so hard. I knew the author Helen Fielding when I was younger and realised how much she is like her character. Bridget reminded me of myself, too.

The best thing in my garden is a banana plant. It looks so tropical and, although I don't expect to grow any bananas, I use the leaves to wrap fish in before baking the parcel in the oven, oriental style. So it's not just ornamental, it's practical, too.

Madonna is a tremendously talented performer. I like almost everything she's ever done and I'm a big fan of her album Ray Of Light. I also loved her version of American Pie — it's rare to hear such an excellent cover. She's such a strong, independent woman and a great mother with a sharp business brain.

I need heat to unwind and always choose to take my holidays in hot countries. Barbados is my favourite. I'll head to The Croc Bar in the evenings. It's a bar in a tin shack and everyone on the island knows it. It plays great Caribbean music, serves the smoothest rum and always has a wonderful, relaxed atmosphere.

The Sixth Sense is a great film starring Bruce Willis, who is one of my favourite movie stars. I usually fidget during films, but I got completely immersed in this one.

My favourite shop is Harvey Nichols. All my favourite designers and perfume counters are there, so I can buy lots under one roof.

I've started to do a lot more shopping on the internet because it's so convenient. I like amazon.com best, though. I browse around the site just as I would a bookshop. I bought an antiques guide as a birthday present for a friend and I also buy books for the kids.

I watch all the soaps. I like the humour in Coronation Street and the village life in Emmerdale. But if I had to choose one I liked most, it would be EastEnders. There's always something exciting happening in Albert Square. Peggy, played by Barbara Windsor, is my absolute favourite character.

Jamie Theakston

Jamie's a football fan who's into Egyptian hieroglyphics and the smell of freshly-cut grass

I have a passion for ancient Egyptian hieroglyphics. I travelled to a burial tomb on a camel to film a series for the BBC education team. I was blown away by how beautiful and intricate the lettering and paintings are. It was a real eye-opener.

I love the smell of freshly-cut grass and was always keen to get the Flymo out at my mum's on a Sunday afternoon. There's something special about handling cut grass, too, especially if it's slightly wet.

I fell in love with an album called Blue Lines by Massive Attack. It was the only tape I had with me when I once drove to the Monaco Grand Prix. My friend and I knew the words backwards by the time we got there. It's my favourite album.

I spent one New Year's Eve in Reykjavik in Iceland and had a brilliant time getting rather drunk. I'd been there the year before and thought the place was so cool, I just had to go back for a big national holiday when everyone goes totally crazy. It's such a fantastic, trendy city, full of nice geysers.

I absolutely love pigging out on Vesta Beef Curry. Just thinking about it makes me salivate and, thankfully, it's one of those dishes that isn't too spicy, so I usually make loads and stick it in the fridge for anyone else who happens to be dropping in that day. I love roast beef, even though it can be a bit dodgy eating too much of it these days.

Des Lynam is the ultimate TV professional. I've never forgotten how cool he was when the Grand National was called off because of the IRA bomb scare.

When I was a schoolboy, I was really into Roy Of The Rovers. I still have about 12 of the annuals and my favourite is the 1973 edition. It was a particularly good year – the picture captions are really funny.

I've always been a bit of a Sony PlayStation nut, I'm afraid, and one of my favourite games is called Wipeout. I can't really describe what it's about except to say that it's a driving-a-spaceship type of game. It's totally insane, very fast and very furious.

Liza Tarbuck

Rock pools, collecting glass ashtrays, Stansted Airport... these are a few of Liza's favourite things

The Larry Sanders Show is head and shoulders above any other comedy. The brilliance of the writing and acting as they send up the American chat show is a pleasure to behold. It makes a mockery of the cliché that Yanks don't get satire.

Rock pools have always been treasure chests to me. I think most kids are fascinated by the living things they find in them. I played in them all the time as a child.

I always wear Bulgari perfume – it's a really beautiful, soft fragrance. I try to stock up on it whenever I'm in a tax-free shop at an airport because it's quite pricey stuff.

My favourite building is Stansted Airport, designed by Sir Norman Foster. Like all great buildings, it has a beautiful way of using natural light. I've always been fascinated by architecture and even designed my first flat.

As a young girl I was fascinated by the children's TV show Tales Of The Riverbank, which used real animals to tell the stories. It must have been responsible for lots of pet hamsters getting jammed tight into floating Tupperware boxes by their owners. Maybe that's why it doesn't get repeated – the animal rights people would have a field day.

I've been doing pilates for years and it helps you breathe better. It was pioneered in POW camps because they didn't have enough food to do heavy exercise.

I have a collection of glass ashtrays. I don't know why – maybe it's again because of my slight obsession with the use of light and reflection. As a kid, I was really into crystals and collecting stones.

I love dogs with big fat necks, especially Staffordshire bull terriers. They're really safe for kids and you can have a good play with them around their mouths and ears.

I used to have a really big crush on Spanish golfer Severiano Ballesteros. He was a great player and he's damn sexy! My father used to play quite a lot of pro-celeb stuff with Seve, so it wasn't long before I had his poster stuck on my bedroom wall.

Lorraine Bracco

Bette Davis is my favourite actress. When I saw Now, Voyager, I thought: 'I want to do that!' Her transformation from ugly duckling to beautiful swan is something I once dreamed of.

Montgomery Clift is great in A Place In The Sun. The chemistry between him and Elizabeth Taylor in the film is electric. The close-ups of them together just make me shout: 'Oh, my God!'

I'd like to meet Jesus Christ and ask him: 'What the hell happened?' We've been killing people and hurting people for centuries in the name of God and in the name of Jesus. I'd love to know what his explanation would be.

I know I'm in it, but I never miss The Sopranos. Even though I know what's going to happen, the fabulous thing is it still manages to surprise me when I tune in. I'm so proud to be a part of the show.

I love artichokes. You can cook them any way you want and I'll eat them. I'm just crazy for them.

My brother had an old record of Chubby Checker's The Twist and he taught me how to do the dance. He was better than me – he could do the double time and I couldn't.

I'm a real-estate whore. I love buying properties, fixing them up, then selling them on. I mainly buy places in New York because that's the area I know best – and it's an amazing city.

Morocco is magnificent to visit. I love everything about the place – the food, the people, the colours, the smells – everything. It's my favourite place in the world and I've been at least 15 times.

I'm really into Bikram Yoga. It's a really tough form of yoga because they heat up the room to about 100 degrees and you do the postures and exercises for 90 minutes. It's hard, but it's a great work-out.

I would love to play Blanche DuBois in A Streetcar Named Desire. I'd be happy to play anything by Tennessee Williams, though, because I love the way he wrote his female characters.

John Hannah

John snowboards because it's dangerous, adores mushrooms and looks up to Johnny Depp

It's A Wonderful Life with James Stewart is my absolute favourite film. I watch it when I want to feel good, particularly at Christmas. I was away last Christmas and took a copy with me because you can't always trust they'll show it on TV when you're abroad.

Snowboarding is a hobby. My friend, the actor Liev Schreiber, and I were in Canada and getting a bit competitive because there's nothing else to do but get sporty. So we took up snowboarding. It's kind of dangerous, but that's part of the point.

I hate having to travel on the underground in London. I get tube rage. Everyone piles on while you're trying to get off. I tripped someone up the other day when they pushed into me.

When I was growing up, I tried never to miss an episode of The Sweeney. I liked it when the villains got off. It seemed to give it more of a sense of reality. That doesn't tend to happen in TV cop shows now, but then how can you tell who the real villains are today anyway?

I used to love Roxy Music. My sister had a copy of Bryan Ferry's These Foolish Things album when I was a child. It was the first time I'd really taken any notice of music. Roxy Music had split up by the time I got into them, so I went and discovered all their early stuff for myself.

Johnny Depp's an actor I've really admired for a long time. Not just in terms of the way he works, but also because of the choices he's made over the years. He always walks his own path. He's great.

I love mushroom season in France. When I've been there, I've had some wonderful cep mushrooms. I could eat bucket loads of them.

I play a lot of golf in summer. Tiger Woods has been great for the game in every way. Hopefully, he's an inspiration to all young golfers. Really, I'd like to see more young Scottish golfers coming through.

Barcelona is somewhere I always look forward to visiting. I really enjoy standing and looking at all those amazing buildings.

Lulu

The first really big influence on me was Ray Charles singing the blues. My father used to get angry about what he called Ray's 'moaning', but I'd still listen to him all the time as I found I preferred black American music to white British music.

I've always been a Glasgow Rangers fan. But I don't follow the team's fortunes as much as those of Sir Alex Ferguson, who used to play for them. I think he's a fellow Scot of real integrity.

I'm passionate about the John Miles song Music, which was a big hit in the 70s. I especially identify with the line: 'Music was my first love and it will be my last.' I think that song sums up my whole life, too.

I really loved the film Maverick, even though I'm not usually crazy about Westerns. The movie has a very modern feel and Mel Gibson is a hugely underrated comic actor, while I've always been a great fan of Jodie Foster.

I'm a strong believer in star signs and have read many books on my sign, **Scorpio.** We Scorpios are supposed to be very passionate with a dark, self-destructive side – just think of how the scorpion stings itself to death. Three is my lucky number because I was born on 3 November.

Adam Ant was one of my favourite pop stars, although my son Jordan used to be an even bigger fan. I once had an Adam Ant outfit, complete with tricorn hat and puffed sleeves, made to measure for Jordan as a present. He loved it.

Dusty Springfield was not only a dear friend, she was also a huge inspiration to me. When she left The Springfields to go solo, she was the first woman to demonstrate girl power. She was such a powerful force and yet vulnerable, with a voice that really bared her soul.

Ever since having a car crash years ago, I've been a regular visitor to my chiropractor. Luckily, mine is very gentle with me because I've heard a lot of them can really crack your joints to put you back on track. I've found going there has been a terrific experience.

Mariah Carey

It's important to Mariah to protect her voice so the singer loves honey and hates smoking. Her favourite food is pasta

As my voice is so delicate, I have always cherished the fresh air, particularly in Central Park, which is a vital green area for New Yorkers. I'm now actually a spokeswoman for a charity called the New York Fresh Air Fund.

I love fresh bagels with a salmon and cheese filling. I survived on a diet of iced tea and bagels when I first moved to New York. Those were the days when sometimes I only had $5 to live on for the week, so my friends and I befriended a deli guy who would give us free tea and bagels.

I'm a fan of The Sound of Music by Rodgers and Hammerstein and I was lucky enough to play the role of Maria when I was younger. I thought Julie Andrews was brilliant in the film and I love that image of her running over the mountain tops.

My favourite food is Italian, especially pasta. I have to eat it in moderation, though, or I'd get fat. My ex-husband Tommy Mottola was a wonderful cook and he taught me a lot about traditional Italian dishes.

I've always eaten lots of honey, which is something my mother taught me. She used to train opera singers, so I soon found out that honey can be very good protection for my voice – as well as tasting delicious on toast.

I hate the smell of cigarette smoke, even though I used to smoke myself. I began at 12, but quit when I was 17 because it was ruining my voice. I shy away from nightclubs because of the smoke and, even when I sing live, I make sure there isn't too much dry ice because my voice is affected by such things.

Aretha Franklin is my biggest idol and I listen to her music constantly. I was once asked to sing a cover of her hit Natural Woman, but her version is so untouchable that I decided not to do it. I've seen her several times in concert, but I was always afraid to be introduced to her because I know I'd just be at a total loss for words.

I adore butterflies. After moving into my apartment, I began to collect lots of things with butterfly designs.

Jonathan Ross

Jonathan's perfect evening would be reading superhero comics and eating Branston Pickle straight from the jar

Even though the supermodel thing has died down a bit, I still think Naomi Campbell is absolutely gorgeous. We all have our own favourite, but I just think that Naomi was the face of the 90s.

Comic magazines have always been my first love. My wife Jane used to get a bit concerned when she'd ask me if I was coming to bed and I'd say: 'I won't be long, I'm just looking at Captain America.' I've always loved superheroes.

I have a soft spot for clothes by designer Thierry Mugler. Through the years, I've attracted quite a lot of publicity because of my choice of suits. I used to love wearing my Mugler suits. They're a really nice cut.

I've always loved the 'White Album' by The Beatles. When Paul McCartney appeared on my old TV show The Last Resort many years ago, he signed my copy in black felt-tip pen. Now it looks fab hanging on my wall.

Actor Steve Martin is my all-time hero. When I interviewed him, I was so in awe I thought I was going to make a complete fool of myself. I giggled all the way through it because he was really chatty.

I'm a coffee-holic, getting through at least 15 cups a day. I used to read Coffee Lovers magazine because I'd become something of a connoisseur of good-quality coffee beans.

It was Akira Kurosawa and the whole samurai thing that first ignited my burning love for Asian cinema. The first Korean film I saw was Oldboy. It's got a great story and satisfies on every level.

I love the taste of Branston Pickle. I have it on everything. I just spoon it over my food. If I come in late at night feeling hungry, I've been known to eat it straight from the jar.

I've been attracted to Florida for years, although I don't think I could ever live there full time. For a start, there are more than 160 TV channels, but nothing really worth watching on any of them. I do love being able to take my surfboard across the road to the ocean to catch some small waves.

Kerry Katona

Kerry thinks there's nothing better than having a good gossip and enjoys a night at home with a takeaway chicken curry

Rod Stewart is my hero. If you ask me what's No1, I won't be able to tell you. I'm happier playing my Rod hits. The Killing Of Georgie and Tonight's The Night are my faves.

You can't beat a long glass of cool milk. I've always loved it from when I was a child and used to drink loads of the stuff.

Actor Hugh Grant is hilarious. His dancing sequence in Love Actually is what makes it a fantastic film.

I order takeaway chicken curries at least twice a week. I absolutely love them. I'd make them myself, but I think takeaway ones taste better.

The book PS, I Love You by Cecelia Ahern, the Irish PM's daughter, is both funny and sad. It's a novel based on letters from a dying man to his wife, written for her to read after his death to help her cope without him.

I'm absolutely dying to have a crack at Strictly Come Dancing – it's a real passion of mine. My mum and I used to watch all the films like Flashdance and Dirty Dancing. I love all that salsa stuff.

I adore gossiping – that's why appearing on the TV show Loose Women was the best job in the world. I can't believe they paid me to go on TV and just do what I love doing anyway – talk, talk, talk.

Pirates Of The Caribbean has all those wonderful period dresses and, of course, it also has Johnny Depp. What more could you possibly want from a movie?

Palma in Majorca is the best place for holidays. I've rented villas with friends and been to all the English restaurants and karaoke nights. It's a British holiday abroad.

I love Jade Goody. Since Big Brother 3, she has juggled the opening of a beauty salon, her media career and the launch of a perfume. I saw her TV show Just Jade and she's brilliant.

I was distraught when Friends ended. I bawled my eyes out. I felt like Ross, Rachel, Joey, Chandler, Monica and Phoebe were my real friends.

Jon Bon Jovi

Wild man of rock Jon loves Hillary Clinton, riding his Harley-Davidson, watching The Godfather and playing golf

In 1992 I took some time off from the band and rode my Harley-Davidson across America, playing rhythm guitar for a friend of mine, Southside Johnny. It was wonderful just getting on the bike each day and I earned $20 a day playing small bars. Great memories!

Bruce Springsteen is my idol. His album Born To Run changed my life. He's an inspirational figure to any fellow New Jerseyite. We've become great friends over the years and he's joined me and my band on stage to sing a few old tunes.

I love playing music, but the minute this is just nostalgia, Bon Jovi will pack up their guitars. If it's fat guys pulling up their tight jeans, then I'm out. Until then, I can't stop.

I'm a great fan of Hillary Clinton. I know her and her husband quite well now, having performed with the band for them about six times. She loves me – she's a huge fan of ours – and I think she's terrific.

My favourite film of all time has to be The Godfather because I'm from a very traditional Italian family myself. I've had the pleasure of meeting Robert De Niro several times and he has a magical personality.

The combination of rock stars and golf means only one thing – too much time on our hands. I picked up the game while we were on the road. It takes up the whole day. You're out in nature, walking around, and that's good. I try not to break too many things or hit too many people.

The Sopranos is my favourite TV series. I even have a Sopranos shirt. The show also stars my old friend Steve Van Zandt, Bruce Springsteen's original guitarist – a wonderful actor.

I loved playing Sarah Jessica Parker's lover in Sex And The City. We had a great time shooting it over two very hot days in June.

I'm a big fan of artist Andy Warhol and I think he had a huge impact on the 20th century. His work was so vibrant and I'm lucky enough to have his Superman logo on my wall and also two limited-edition James Dean prints.

Mariella Frostrup

Husky-voiced Mariella enjoys deep-sea diving and indulging her taste for expensive caviar

I love deep-sea diving. It's the best way to pass the time on holiday if, like me, you really hate sunbathing. I went diving off the coast of Costa Rica and there were hammerhead sharks everywhere. It was an exhilarating experience and now I'm hooked.

It may be ridiculously expensive, but I get terrible cravings for caviar. At £90 a tin, it's given me some rather large credit card bills in the past, but to hell with the cost.

Going to the movies and eating popcorn is my favourite pastime. When I used to present the Little Picture Show, I'd go to six film screenings a week, which was great because I was getting paid to do something I love. My favourite films of all time are Apocalypse Now and The Return Of The Pink Panther. One of my heroes is the actor Ralph Fiennes because he's mean, moody and, I'm sure, totally impossible in real life.

I love popping over for shopping trips to New York – the Donna Karan store is my favourite. I used to be very insecure about my body, convinced that I was fat, short and had tiny breasts and a big bum – so I was never confident about buying clothes. I still wish I had bigger breasts and longer legs.

Some of my closest friends live in Tuscany and I'd love to spend half the year there. Much as I enjoy living in London, I do feel the need to escape into the great outdoors.

The GMTV presenter Penny Smith and I book ourselves into a health farm once a year and get fully pampered. I love being really indulged, even though I do allow myself to smoke the odd cigarette.

I own a silver Vespa, which is very trendy for bombing around London. It's a pleasure to use because you don't get stuck in traffic. Better still, no one recognises me in a crash helmet.

I can spend all day hunting out a bargain on the antiques stalls at Portobello Road Market, near where I live. However, some of the stallholders may take the mickey out of me for being a panellist once on Going For A Song.

Julien Macdonald

Fashion designer Julien adores style icon Marilyn Monroe, has 25 John Smedley jumpers and jets off to Rio

Karl Lagerfeld's a living legend in fashion. I was one of his protégés at Chanel and he taught me to follow my own intuition. He's one of my favourite designers and a great man.

Let Me Love You by US R&B star Mario is a song I can't get out of my head. I bought his album Turning Point as well.

Jo Malone Lime, Basil & Mandarin Cologne is my signature scent. It's fresh and sexy. Whenever I wear it, people always ask me: 'What's that gorgeous smell?'

Gentlemen Prefer Blondes is a film I could watch over and over again. Marilyn Monroe is my favourite style icon of all time. She was daring and wasn't afraid of her femininity.

Sex And The City is still my top TV show. I'm a huge fan of Samantha because she was sex-mad and full of fun. I've dressed Kim Cattrall on screen and in real life.

The Moroccan city of Marrakech is amazing. Once you've been to the souk, you'll never forget the smell of its hot spices, the hustle and bustle of the place and the sheer indulgence of the people over there.

The Rio Carnival in Brazil is my ultimate holiday destination. It's a week-long indulgence of partying, fun, colour and glamour – a great place.

John Smedley jumpers are my style staple. I own around 25 in various styles and shades and I'm a regular at the London flagship store.

The Alchemist by Paulo Coelho is a very special book. It's dreamy and romantic and tells a story of love in a faraway place.

I love glamorous things. I love fur because it keeps you warm and it's sexy. There's nothing better than seeing a woman slip off a fox or mink coat and underneath there's a skimpy, strapless little dress.

I think cosmetic surgery is great. Anything that can transform your life for the better is a great advancement. I'm going to get wrinkles, so as soon as I'm ready, I'll be first in the queue. I'll have everything done!

Martine McCutcheon

Martine is a Manchester United fan, adores her mum and enjoys beach holidays in Tenerife

Boxing's how I work out. I do a version of it called boxercise at my local gym. It's like the real thing – only you don't actually land any punches. I work up a real sweat and always feel raring to go afterwards.

I love Tenerife. It's where I had my first real holiday when I was 16. I went with a friend and we spent every night in the clubs, with our bikinis under our clothes so we could go straight to the beach to sleep it off and get a tan.

I believe totally in Tarot cards because whenever I've used them they've always come true. I'm curious about the future and my mum reads the cards for me. She doesn't know how to do them properly, so she looks things up in a book, which makes it more of a laugh.

I've always loved singing. I used to be in an all-girl teen band called Milan. We toured with East 17, which was great. Our record company got rid of us after a couple of singles.

Audrey Hepburn is my role model. I can watch her in Breakfast At Tiffany's over and over again. It's about an ordinary girl who wants to become someone. I really identify with that. It's ironic I ended up playing Tiffany in EastEnders.

I enjoy a drink, but I can't stand vodka. It makes me go all emotional and I start crying and telling people I love them. Everyone suddenly becomes my best friend.

My mum Jenny is brilliant. My dad left us when I was a baby and for the first nine years of my life she brought me up. She was only 19 when she had me, but she always put my needs before her own. I owe her a lot.

I used to play soccer and I still love it. I got taken to Arsenal to see my first match when I was eight. I support Manchester United now. When I'm in Scotland, I follow Celtic, which really annoys my stepdad John – he's a Rangers fan.

I can't stand drugs and would never take them. I've had people try to sell me ecstasy and they look at you strangely if you say no. Just because others do it, I don't see why I should, too.

Richard Bacon

Presenter and Radio DJ Richard has a soft spot for Yorkshire terriers, loves snooker and harboured ambitions to be an MP

I've been a snooker fan ever since I was a youngster trying, without much luck, to make a reasonable break. I still play the odd frame with friends and enjoy watching top players on the telly.

Citizen Kane is my favourite film. Orson Welles has such presence as Kane, the newspaper tycoon who dies leaving his last words to be deciphered by a reporter.

I had a great time at the Cannes Film Festival when I was doing interviews for The Big Breakfast down on the beach. One day, we tried to get some locals to do a streak for the cameras and it was hilarious watching the producer trying to ask them in French.

An early ambition of mine was to be an MP and sit in the House of Commons. I still scan the political coverage in the papers, but these days I never seem to go far beyond The Times crossword.

I think Morgan Freeman is a great leading character actor. I can't think of a better role than the one he plays in The Shawshank Redemption. It's a great tale about a wrongly convicted man in prison and is told in the most uplifting way.

I've always had a soft spot for Yorkshire terriers because they're an ideal family dog. Growing up with my two sisters Juliet and Helena, we had lots of fun with our terrier Scamper.

My favourite album is Revolver by The Beatles, released in the summer of 1966. The Swinging Sixties were at their height and songs like Yellow Submarine and Eleanor Rigby provided the soundtrack.

When I was younger, I had aspirations to be a great sax player. But I was rubbish. I also tried to master the piano and drums, but didn't get very far.

My comic hero has to be the wonderful Steve Coogan. I just can't stop laughing whenever I see him doing Alan Partridge. Just check out the video of Steve Coogan Live: The Man Who Thinks He's It to see why the audience is in stitches.

Mary J Blige

R&B diva Mary has a passion for shoes, loves to decorate new homes and says reading the Bible changed her life

I really admire Serena and Venus Williams – I'm so proud of what they've achieved. They are both great role models for the younger generation of African-Americans.

I'm hopelessly addicted to shoes. Jimmy Choo, Plein Sud and Marc Jacobs all make beautiful footwear. I've got special rooms just for my shoes and I can't help splashing out when I spy a gorgeous new pair.

Chaka Khan is definitely one of my musical inspirations. Vocally, she's like heaven as far as I'm concerned. She's got the whole package and is a fantastic performer.

The Bible really changed my life. It made me realise that we all have a long way to go before we stop being selfish and spiteful – and I'm trying to become a better person. I don't get to read it every day, but I set aside time whenever I can.

Who Wants To Be A Millionaire? is great. I love the trivia and I actually learn a lot from watching the show. I sit in front of the TV on my own and try to figure out the answers. I'm shockingly good and am often quite surprised that I know more than I thought I did.

I've become a real whizz at interior designing. When I moved into my first apartment, I caught the decorating bug. I love planning colour schemes and deciding which accessories I'll use in each room. No one knows my taste better than I do, so each room reflects a part of me.

I adore the smell of cooked rice. It reminds me of when I was a little kid watching my mum cook. Every time I smell it, I know that there must be some chicken just waiting around the corner.

The Caribbean island of Aruba is the most gorgeous place I've been to. It was the first vacation my husband and I took and I fell in love with it. It's so beautiful and unspoilt.

Scarface is one of my favourite movies. I used to see scenes like that on a daily basis when growing up in New York. Now it's more like a comedy – there are so many one-liners, I can't help but laugh.

Natalie Cassidy

Actress Natalie loves sipping Del Boy-style cocktails and her most precious souvenir is an Oasis tambourine

I'm really into the Adrian Mole books by Sue Townsend. I've read most of them – The Secret Diary, Growing Pains and True Confessions – about eight times each. I particularly love the character of Bert Baxter, the old bloke who smokes Woodbines.

My favourite album is (What's The Story) Morning Glory? by Oasis. I bought it when I was 12 and every song on it means something special to me. I was at the front at one of their concerts at Wembley and I caught Liam Gallagher's tambourine.

I'd love to go to Barbados again. I once went with a friend and his family to a resort near St James. It was quite a posh part, but everyone was really friendly, especially the beach boys and the barmen.

I really admire Martin Luther King. I did a project on him at school about how he changed people's ideas of race in America and helped to end segregation. It's great that he taught people to stand up for themselves.

My dream is to work with Kathy Burke. She is really funny and even though she's got loads of money and fame, she's still down-to-earth. If I ever did great films like her, I'd still want to be normal and go to the local supermarket to do my shopping.

I like a Jack Daniel's and Coke. I also really love Planet Hollywood's non-alcoholic cocktails – the really huge ones with umbrellas and fruit, just like the ones Del Boy drinks.

The best moment of my career was when I was 17 and Graham Norton came up to me at the Soap Awards. He could hardly speak and was sort of gasping and spluttered: 'As soon as you're 18, you've got to come on my show. You're my favourite.' He seemed starstruck, which was really weird as I'm a huge fan of his.

I must be one of the few girls who doesn't fancy Matt Damon, but my favourite film is Good Will Hunting. It's funny and sad and philosophical, but I like it because Matt Damon and Ben Affleck wrote the script themselves and starred in it. That's something I'd love to do sometime in the future.

Lennox Lewis

Ex-world heavyweight boxing champion Lennox is an X Files fanatic and has a thing about rum and raisin ice cream

I've read lots of biographies about my hero Muhammad Ali. I'll never forget sitting down with my brother Dennis to watch Ali fight Joe Frazier back in the 70s. It was a totally inspiring moment.

I think Halle Berry is very possibly the most beautiful woman in the world. She's also a great actress, as anyone who saw her in X-Men will testify.

The Celestine Prophecy by James Redfield is a wonderful read. It's an adventure story set in the rainforests of Peru, which tries to explain the meaning of life as revealed in an ancient manuscript.

I've always loved rum and raisin ice cream. Before I retired, when I was in training for a fight, I had to stay away from it and went on a strict exercise and diet regime.

I love that old Yellow Pages TV commercial in which the guy wakes up to find that his parents' home has been totally wrecked by the party he held there the night before. The look on his face when he sees the pair of glasses someone's drawn in felt-tip pen on the painting is hilarious.

I never get bored watching repeats of The X Files. I love the show, primarily because I've always been fascinated by programmes about science and nature.

I'm a big fan of Des'ree and I think Feel So High is a brilliant record. She's got such a fabulous, soulful voice and I think that song will still be played for many years to come.

Jamaica's such a beautiful country and I visit the island as often as possible. There can't be many better ways to spend an afternoon than chilled out on the beach with Bob Marley tunes playing in the background.

Al Pacino has to be my favourite actor, especially in the role of Tony Montana in the brilliant gangster movie Scarface. Although the film is almost three hours long, watching Tony go completely bonkers in fabulous Miami is great viewing.

Natalie Imbruglia

Diving isn't just Natalie's hobby, it also features in her favourite film and she loves the Cayman Islands

I love being driven around in Mini Coopers in British racing green. I especially like the ones that come with walnut dashboards and black or red interiors.

I'm really into wearing Levi's and my favourite jeans are definitely the original Orange Tab variety. They're quite 70s, really, which is cool because I love the clothes and music from that period.

My favourite drink is vodka with cranberry juice. It tastes wonderful and, for some reason, the cranberry helps you avoid getting a bad hangover. If you're in a cocktail bar, ask for a Sea Breeze – it's basically the same thing but with lime in it.

Scuba diving is a big passion. I had a brilliant time learning how to do it properly in the Cayman Islands and now my idea of paradise is to stay on a boat with a live-in sushi chef and to go scuba diving every day. Heaven.

The Big Blue is my all-time favourite film. It's a story about how two deep-sea divers compete against each other to see how deep they can go underwater without air. Oh, and they rescue a dolphin.

The CD I can't stop playing is Radiohead's OK Computer, which features the wonderful vocals of Thom Yorke. My favourite track is No Surprises and I also love the video to Street Spirit. It's brilliant.

I love Africa, especially the plains of Kenya. It was the first holiday I took after leaving Neighbours and it's a beautiful continent but with terrible poverty. When I got back, I decided to send money to support a girl who lived in a mud hut near Nairobi.

I fell in love with Notting Hill when I moved to the UK in 1994. London is an exciting, international place with people from different countries and classes. I've visited Portobello Road Market so much, my friends called me Notting Hill Nat.

As a little girl, my Mickey Mouse doll was the first thing in my life to which I felt emotionally attached. I took the little fella absolutely everywhere and would play with him all the time.

148

Minnie Driver

London-born Minnie loves curried chicken and her Cartier silver watch, but she misses England when she's in the US

My favourite building is probably the Victoria and Albert Museum in London. The ancient Asian sculptures and the costume gallery are my favourites. I really could spend hours looking at all the exhibits.

I'm passionate about music and love early Bruce Springsteen and Joni Mitchell albums. In particular, Born To Run by Springsteen is so full of evocative poetry and wonderfully epic music.

One of my favourite possessions is a silver Cartier tank watch. It was a gift from actor Josh Brolin. It's really lovely and I never take it off.

Maybe because I grew up in Barbados, I've always been a sucker for cocktails laced with rum. The best is a slug of rum served with sugar, lots of ice and freshly-squeezed lime juice.

My favourite meal is an Indian curried chicken with mango chutney on the side and a nice green salad. I'm a big chicken fan anyway, but this is the most delicious way to eat it.

Seeing Meryl Streep in Sophie's Choice inspired me to become an actress. I'd never seen acting like that before and it got me thinking that I could be up there, too, just like Meryl.

I was fortunate to star on screen with some gorillas once and it was amazing – especially when the babies came up and tried to tear my hand off. After such an incredible experience, I think they have to be my favourite animal now.

I still miss London, in spite of the weather – every six weeks or so, I fly over from the US to spend time with friends and family. Luckily, none of them have anything to do with making movies, so it's great to hang out, drink tea and chat about normal, everyday things.

I've always been really into playing golf because it's a great way to relax and take a stroll in the sunshine. Growing up, I was lucky enough to play at The Royal Westmoreland Golf and Country Club course in Barbados, which has to be the most beautiful golf course in the world.

Max Beesley

Actor Max is a James Bond fan, enjoys French food and relaxes with a four-pack of Budweiser

I adore French food and Raymond Blanc's restaurant Le Manoir Aux Quatre Saisons in Oxfordshire is unbeatable. I went there once to attend his week-long cooking school, which was fascinating. I make a mean soufflé now!

I'm a massive Manchester United fan and in particular I admire Ryan Giggs. I think his manager Sir Alex Ferguson has been like a father to him and it's great to see how he's matured, both as a person and as a footballer.

I've always been bonkers about 007. Dr No is my favourite because it features Ursula Andress emerging from the sea – on a beach in Jamaica on which I've actually stayed.

New York is probably my favourite city to holiday in because there's such a great energy about Manhattan. I usually stay around SoHo, near the Guggenheim Museum on Broadway.

I was really starstruck when I met Burt Reynolds in 2001 while we were making a film together. I bought him a vodka and he spent the next hour telling me lots of amazing stories about hanging out with people like Frank Sinatra.

The Firm by John Grisham is definitely my favourite read. It's a fascinating book and is a real insight into just how corrupt some American corporations can be.

I really love rap music and the Wu-Tang Clan in particular. I think it's amazing how rap has become the biggest-selling musical genre in America, even though so much of it is officially censored.

There's nothing nicer than relaxing with a four-pack of Budweiser. I've always preferred lager to any other alcohol. Maybe it's because I'm a bit of a traditional northern lad.

King Street in Manchester is my favourite street in the whole world and I like hanging about in DKNY and Starbucks. I love going home so much because it really gets your feet back on the ground and gives you a sense of belonging.

Victoria Wood

Victoria has a passion for the piano, adores close pal Julie Walters and has always admired Joyce Grenfell

I first saw Joyce Grenfell when I was six and she's been a huge influence on me ever since. Joyce used to do a two-hour stage show with just a man at the piano. She made me realise I might get away with it, too.

I don't enjoy getting stopped in the street and being a celebrity, so I'd hate to be on This Is Your Life. My shyness has improved over the years, but it wouldn't stand up to appearing with Michael Aspel and the big red book. I'd die.

I'm a great believer in natural childbirth. I wanted it for my first child Grace, but I ended up having an epidural. I got my own way with Henry, though. When I screamed the place down, the midwife told me to be quiet. I just said: 'I don't care.'

I love railways, especially steam trains. There's something romantic about travelling by rail to far-flung places. I went on a Great Railway Journey from Crewe for the BBC and it was good fun.

The piano has been a wonderful escape for me for as long as I can remember. As a kid, I used to have lessons but stopped going because I preferred playing on my own. When my parents came home, I'd slam down the lid and pretend I hadn't been playing. They knew, of course.

I don't go to therapy now, but it's a good way of releasing things. I'm confident on stage, but I used to find it difficult to be assertive in real life. It was like getting a car fixed. I went to an expert and, when it was mended, I left.

Julie Walters and I first met as students at Manchester Polytechnic's School of Theatre and we've been close friends ever since. Our sense of humour is the same and whenever we meet up, every few weeks or so, we just take up where we left off.

I loathe dresses. I've never been seen in one and I don't intend to start now. I'm very much a jeans and trousers person. I've been known to go out in a skirt, even though they make me look like a netball teacher – but the only time I've put on a dress was in private and I looked silly.

Nelly Furtado

Singer Nelly has a thing about London's street markets and is never without her trainers

I have a real passion for the vibe of London's street markets. I love the better known ones such as Camden and Portobello, which sell great retro clothing. But I'm just as at home at local markets, where you can buy beautiful flowers and vegetables.

I think Jude Law's amazing. He's captivating on screen and very sexy, too. My favourite film of his is eXistenZ, directed by David Cronenberg. It's about a virtual-reality game in which players have their nervous systems linked to a hi-tech pod that alters their reactions to fear, needs and desires.

I love Asian Dub Foundation. They're one of my favourite British groups – a real kick-ass band with great songs.

My favourite place to relax for a couple of weeks would be Ponta Delgada in San Miguel, which is a small island in the Azores almost 1,000 miles west of Portugal. My parents Maria and Antonio live there and it's just the most beautiful volcanic island, full of hot springs and exotic wildlife.

I wear Angel by Thierry Mugler. It's a very hippy-dippy smell like chocolate and I love the bottle it comes in, too. My second choice would be one of The Body Shop's beautiful body sprays.

I wear a lot of trainers, but my special favourites were my Adidas shell toes. I liked them so much that I wore them when I appeared on the American shows Jay Leno and Saturday Night Live.

Mother Teresa was perhaps the person I found most inspiring. That someone with so much spirituality, modesty and inner beauty should have lived in this day and age was a rare thing. She was the nearest we had to a modern-day saint.

I love living in Toronto – it's the most multicultural city in the entire world. There are hundreds of languages spoken and you can be anything you want in Toronto. The other great thing about it is that it's a city where gay marriage is legal. Grassroots political activism is encouraged and easy to find. I feel grounded when I'm there.

James Nesbitt

James Nesbitt serenades women with a particular Beatles song and doesn't like Paul Newman's salad dressing

Paul Newman really fascinates me. I've read many biographies on the great man, as well as seeing many of his films. But my best tip is never, ever buy his salad dressing. It's not much cop and it kind of demeans his status as one of the great actors.

Windsor House in Belfast is my favourite building in the world – even if it's a bit banal and bizarre. It's the first skyscraper to be built in Northern Ireland. It was put up in the 50s and it's an incredible structure.

Till There Was You by The Beatles is the song that means the most to me. I've sung it to just about every woman I've ever made a play for. Usually, by about halfway through, I know if I'm going to get off with them or not.

I spent my honeymoon in a place called Positano on the Amalfi Coast in southern Italy. I just fell in love with it. It's so unbelievably romantic and beautiful.

Heaven Can Wait is my all-time favourite film. That's because it's a wonderful, soppy love story. I'm a really big fan of Warren Beatty and Julie Christie anyway and there are some memorable lines that stay with you forever.

I go to a club in Manchester called 5th Avenue. It's full of students and I love it because when the DJ sees me come in, he puts on Teenage Kicks by The Undertones. And I go: 'Cheers, mate! Let's party!'

My golfing handicap is 16 and I'm a proud member of the Royal Portrush Golf Club on Northern Ireland's North Antrim coast. It's one of the greatest golf courses in the world. They used to hold the British Open there – the last time was in 1958 – but now they won't because, sadly, the facilities aren't good enough.

A watch was given to me a few years ago by my mother that belonged to my great uncle David, who I never met. Mum was close to him, but he died quite young of a stroke and I feel her loss of him keenly. It reminds me of Carnlough in County Antrim, where I spent all my childhood holidays, and brings back many happy memories.

Paris Hilton

Paris Hilton is mad about Madonna, has a huge collection of shoes and says celebrating Christmas with her family is very special to her

I'm hopelessly addicted to the TV series Lost. I just can't imagine what it would be like to be stranded on an island like that – it really scares me. I could manage being in Hawaii, where it's filmed, but being there forever would bore me because, although I like chilling out, I prefer to be out doing something.

There are a couple of films I can watch over and over again. I've seen There's Something About Mary 10 times and never got bored with it. Another comedy I find hilarious is Napoleon Dynamite and I've seen that 12 times.

Marilyn Monroe is an icon to so many people around the world. She was an inspiration because she was not only blonde and beautiful, but she was very successful as well. She'll never be forgotten.

I adore the smell of pine needles because it reminds me of lovely family Christmases at home. My mum's a bit of a Christmas freak and over the festive holidays we have five trees around the house, which she loves to decorate.

Like most girls, I'm passionate about shoes. I have so many pairs, it's ridiculous. In fact, I probably have over a thousand pairs and my whole house is like one giant closet because I just put them wherever they'll fit. It's crazy.

I'm so mad about The Immaculate Collection by Madonna, I must have bought it about 10 times over. I love it so much that I take a copy everywhere I go, but I keep losing it, so I have to go out and buy another one. They're all great tracks but Borderline is such a really cool song.

Maneater by Gigi Levangie Grazer is my favourite book. I've also just finished reading The Devil Wears Prada, which is about the fashion industry. It's been made into a film and I can't wait to see it.

My favourite holiday places are the island of Maui in Hawaii and the resort of St Tropez in the south of France. I don't really get left alone in either place, but I love them both so much I still go there. St Tropez especially is like paparazzi hell for me, but it's beautiful.

160

Neil Morrissey

Forget his old lager-swilling Men Behaving Badly image, Neil Morrissey is really a bit of a wine connoisseur

Florians restaurant in Crouch End, North London, is a wonderful place to eat, especially in the garden area during the summer. Both their swordfish and sea bass main courses are a real treat.

I think Loaded magazine brilliantly captures the same kind of mood as Men Behaving Badly did on TV. It was even a bit ahead of its time when it first came out. I think both the magazine and the show were riding the same wave, saying: 'Men drink beer and have a good time – so what?'

It's quite difficult finding a pub in London with a decent pint and a great atmosphere, but The Lansdowne in Primrose Hill is just about perfect. It's also very near home, which is handy if I've had too many and need a lie down.

Des Lynam's a gent and one of TV's true professionals. I met him during filming of the BBC comedy-drama My Summer With Des and thought he was a real charmer. But I reckon anyone that nice has to have a temper. I'd hate to see him lose his.

I must confess I've always been a bit of a Mel Gibson fan, ever since I got my first big break in acting in The Bounty opposite the great man. While we were filming, I pretended to be his brother to pull the girls. Mel didn't mind, he thought it was hysterical.

Actor Adrian Dunbar is probably my best mate. He's best known for starring as the confused showbiz entrepreneur in the film Hear My Song. I first met him at the Guildhall School of Music and Drama. We shared a flat back then.

I like to order cases of the best wines direct from Tuscany in Italy. I love the area because it's so beautiful and also because I'm definitely getting more and more into classy wines these days.

I think Africa is a magical place and I'll never forget my trip to Sudan to raise awareness for the charity War Child. That was in August 1998, when 130 children were dying each day in southern Sudan, yet the people were defiant and proud. It was a very moving experience.

Rachel Stevens

Singer Rachel loves Audrey Hepburn, is a sucker for romantic comedy and adores visiting New York

When I was a kid, it was my dream to go to New York. Then Sex And The City made it look so exciting and bustling. I've got loads of episodes on DVD and when I watch them, it just makes me want to be in Manhattan and visit the theatre and lots of restaurants.

I have a tendency to overdose on cups of tea. I drink it nonstop, but I did force myself to cut down to just three cups a day. It was starting to make me really sluggish, but it was so hard weaning myself off it. I love that caffeine buzz.

David Gray is a brilliant artist. His album White Ladder is one of my favourites. I have a huge collection of CDs. I don't buy them that often but, when I do, I do a bit of an Elton John and get 30 at a time.

I'm a real dog person and I love Weimaraners. They're big silver dogs with sleek coats, blue eyes and they have the loveliest temperament. I used to have a mongrel dog called Rocky, but we had to give him away because I was moving into a flat. It was heartbreaking.

Audrey Hepburn was so beautiful and elegant. I love her style. She was kind of similar to Jackie Onassis with the big glasses and the tailored suits. I've just bought a big black and white print of her in Breakfast At Tiffany's to hang on my bedroom wall.

I'm a sucker for romantic comedies. Notting Hill with Hugh Grant and Julia Roberts is an all-time favourite. I get very slushy and cry a lot – it's best that I'm at home alone when I watch it.

I find it fun to collect all kinds of matchboxes. My favourite is a plastic one I got in LA. It's four times the size of a normal matchbox and has a black and white 50s-style picture of Elvis on the front. It's really cool.

Comedian Lee Evans is the funniest man on the planet. He's just so silly. I started to like him years ago when my girlfriends and I would stay in and watch him over and over again on video. I'm not at all surprised that he packed out Wembley Arena for three nights in a row last December – he's amazing.

Siân Lloyd

With her love of rugby union, male voice choirs and Ty Nant mineral water, it's not difficult to tell that Siân Lloyd is proud to be from Wales

I don't read as much as I should. I love The Go-Between by LP Hartley, but there are so many other books I feel I should read. My mother was in charge of the school library when I was growing up. It meant I was a relatively well-read child – everything from Just William books to CS Lewis's The Chronicles Of Narnia.

For my generation, Nelson Mandela was always that figure in jail for years and years. It was a great joy to see him released. I admire him immensely for all he's done about fighting against apartheid.

Cleaning is so therapeutic and I love my Dyson vacuums. The first one I got was pink. It was almost a prototype version that came out more than a decade ago. I also have one that hangs on the wall, so it's perfect for a small flat.

My sister lives in Paris and I visit her about 10 times a year. I go by Eurostar. Three hours and you save all that time schlepping out to the airports. I'm into green issues, so the fact that I don't use the car appeals to me as well.

I can't stand the drinking water in London. Instead, I prefer Ty Nant, a sparkling Welsh water that comes in beautiful blue bottles. It's expensive, but I loyally ask for it in restaurants. I also like a good dry champagne.

We never had a TV when I was a child and, even now, I don't watch a lot. For sheer professionalism, though, no one can beat Des Lynam as a presenter. He's charming and he has that cool, unflappable nature. I think Des is lovely.

Portmeirion in North Wales, where The Prisoner TV series was filmed, is a magical place. The best party I ever went to was there, when they reopened the hotel after it burnt down. When I get married, I want the ceremony to be in Portmeirion. Failing that, it's where I want the reception.

Rugby union is my sport. I grew up during Wales's glory days in the late 60s and early 70s, when Barry John and Gareth Edwards were playing. I also went out with the captain of the school team, who was the ultimate boyfriend you could have then.

Michael Bublé

Canadian singer Michael has a thing for Soho, Michael Parkinson, playing ice hockey and Jordan

I like women who wear The Body Shop's White Musk. It's such an understated and sexy perfume. Michael by Michael Kors evokes a horrible sexual experience I had once, so even if I meet a stunning woman and she's wearing it, the game's over. But, you know what, just the natural smell of a woman does it for me.

I spend time in Vancouver when I need to get away from it all. I don't get peace and quiet, but there's nowhere I'd rather be than sitting down with my family, having dinner. It's a beautiful city – on the same day that you go swimming in the ocean, you can go skiing in the mountains. It's an incredible place.

The Princess Bride is a great movie. It has everything – action, romance, adventure, loss, heartache. I could watch it a million times. Peter Falk is superb in it.

I love sport and I still play ice hockey. My record company doesn't like me to in case I break my face. I'm a real boy's boy, though – if you have something you can throw and catch, I can make a game of it for hours.

I'm passionate about everything I sing. Stardust is my favourite song of all time and the Black Eyed Peas' Where Is The Love? has a great melody. I love Take That's Back For Good. I just bought their Greatest Hits CD – the girl in the record store recognised me, so I told her it was for my little sister.

Piccadilly Circus is my favourite London stomping ground. My first UK gig was very close by. I also love wandering through Soho. No matter what time of day or night you visit Piccadilly, it's always buzzing.

I adore sushi and have tried making it myself. I'll buy a whole tuna, have it flash frozen, saw off chunks, add soya sauce and wasabi [Japanese horseradish] and I'm happy. Food is my biggest indulgence... or maybe sex. Food with sex would be heaven!

I was addicted to I'm A Celebrity... Get Me Out Of Here!. Jordan was very cute in it. I also think Ricky Tomlinson is a great actor. And, of course, Parkinson is must-see TV. My success in the UK is thanks to Michael's support.

Sheryl Crow

Singer Sheryl loves mature men and dreams of being a champion biker like her all-time hero Steve McQueen

Steve McQueen was truly a hero of the old school. He was flawed, but he represented the American dream and a loss of innocence.

I love Hawaii. I went there with my close friend Stevie Nicks from Fleetwood Mac. We took a catamaran and sailed to the island of Molokai.

I went to see Jerry Springer: The Opera in the West End and I really enjoyed it. It was very funny and quite crazy, just like the TV show.

I'm really into riding motocross bikes, especially off-riding on an automatic starting four-stroke. I grew up riding dirt bikes, so it's kind of in my blood.

I've met Clint Eastwood and his amazingly talented family. We went to see his son Kyle play jazz in a club. Clint looks great for his age. He has a real glint in his eye!

Sean Connery's my favourite James Bond. He may be in his mid-seventies now, but he's still hot. I was fortunate enough to be asked to write the theme tune for Tomorrow Never Dies. There's a great legacy about those movie themes.

I love real music – bands such as The Strokes and The White Stripes. I'm one of those musicians who were developed by the record company before the days of reality TV, so I love bands like these.

My favourite movie is Rushmore and not just because my ex-boyfriend Owen Wilson wrote it. It's about a student who builds an aquarium on the school baseball field. Bill Murray's hilarious in it.

I'm religious about taking my vitamins. I take a fish-oil supplement every single day. I also meditate to create my own pace for the day. I used to get so mad at myself because I couldn't control my frenetic mind. I wasn't able to sit and do nothing. Health begins with a peaceful state of mind.

I love vegetables and fresh food – nothing packaged and nothing with preservatives. I'm eating more vegetables than ever. I also gave up caffeine. I drink decaf coffee instead.

Suranne Jones

Barbados is one of the most memorable places I've ever been to. I went with my Coronation Street co-star Naomi Russell, who played Bobbi. We sat on this amazing beach with a glass of wine each and just gazed out to sea. There was music playing and it was just so incredibly beautiful and serene.

Guys And Dolls is a brilliant film. I'm really into musicals and it's such a classic. It stars Marlon Brando and Frank Sinatra. I played Sarah Brown once and it was one of my favourite roles. It was such a thrill to take part in the stage musical after I'd loved the movie so much. Some of it's set in Havana, Cuba, which I'd love to visit.

Roses are definitely my favourite flowers – they're so romantic. The way to my heart is for someone to send me a red rose. Just one is enough – it says a lot. My boyfriend sent me a single rose and I still have it, dried and kept on my windowsill.

The Beach is one of my all-time favourite books. I'd love to go to Thailand, where it's set. I fancy hanging out on one of those islands. I read the book before I saw the film, which was actually quite disappointing. When you read a book, your imagination can work wonders, but I didn't like the way the film exaggerated things.

Whenever I hear Barry White's You're The First, The Last, My Everything on the radio, I can't help jigging away to it. The words are fantastic as well, so it can make you a bit emotional.

I have a Zippy from Rainbow cuddly toy. It was a present, so I cherish it, but I prefer Bagpuss. I loved him when I was a kid.

I'm fascinated by Marilyn Monroe and Frank Sinatra. I'd love to have been in Hollywood when they were around, just for the drama and glamour of it all and to know the truth about all the dirty deeds that went on in those days. What was the truth about Marilyn's death? And was Frank really a bad guy?

It sounds so awful, but I really like being on my own and not having to answer to anybody. But I love the company of my friends, too.

Moby

Moby – born Richard Melville Hall – is into sci-fi, enjoys drinking tequila, likes to laugh at dogs and grows lavender on his roof

I love northern Arizona because the landscape makes you feel as if you're on another planet. Monument Valley is such a huge area – you can drive for four or five hours and not see any sign of human habitation. It's overwhelming.

This may be very geeky, but I can't live without my Apple iBook. I use it for everything from emailing to writing music and essays. I never leave home without it.

In New York we have these things in parks called dog runs. They're fenced-in areas where you can take your dog and let it off the leash. I love to laugh at the silly things other people's dogs get up to.

Dead Man Walking is probably my all-time favourite film. Tim Robbins' direction is perfect and all the characters are dealt with in an honest way. The scene on death row is one of the most emotionally devastating things I've ever seen.

Patricia Arquette's the sexiest person alive. She's just amazing in the movie True Romance.

My favourite drink is clear tequila on the rocks. I drink it slowly and don't mix it. I can't understand doing quick shots. Why wouldn't you want to savour the taste?

Closer by Joy Division was my favourite record when I was growing up and I've rediscovered it. It's beautiful. I've been really lucky because I've now worked with most of my heroes including New Order.

Freshly cut lavender is the nicest smell on the planet. I have a loft apartment in New York and grow it on my roof deck because it's really resilient. Trimming it is very relaxing.

I'm a bit of a sci-fi geek and for me the best book in the genre is Dune by Frank Herbert. It's been made into a film and a mini series, which were really good. It's such an intricate world that he created.

I own a little vegetarian restaurant in Manhattan called Teany, which I'm passionate about. It's a really small and simple place – not your average celebrity restaurant at all.

Tamzin Outhwaite

The fizz of champagne, the scent of jasmine, and the sound of Joni Mitchell does it for Tamzin

The Maldives are simply idyllic – hundreds of little islands surrounded by their own lagoons. But if you go there, make sure you take loads of books or your boyfriend – not necessarily in that order – because there's nothing to do once you get out of the swimming pool.

A favourite film of mine is Baz Luhrmann's Romeo And Juliet. It obviously wasn't absolutely true to the original play, but it was to its spirit. The soundtrack's amazing, too.

Issey Miyake is my perfume. I first noticed it on a lot of people who are cooler and trendier than me and I decided to buy it. Now I wouldn't wear anything else.

The song River by Joni Mitchell means the most to me. I used to be able to play the guitar years ago and always thought I'd be a folk singer, with my blonde hair and kaftan. The guitar and kaftans are long gone, but River lives on.

I love The Prodigy. They're so in your face. It's great going to their concerts and seeing old green hair Keith Flint do his stuff. I wouldn't want him in my living room, but up on stage no one comes close to him.

Champagne always does the trick – Bollinger, of course, sweetie! If I haven't finished a bottle, I stick a teaspoon in the neck and put it back in the fridge. It works. The bubbles are still there the next time you attack the bottle.

Cate Blanchett is the actress I most admire. She's very raw and natural – everything you expect from a star. There's no pretence, only truth.

The jasmine flower reminds me of Tunisia, where I went the first time I travelled abroad. The scent was everywhere in the air and, even now, a single jasmine blossom makes me yearn to return.

I absolutely love Renault's Mégane Coupé-Cabriolet. In my head, a convertible feels like it could be a lot of hassle, but with this car you literally push a button and from a hard top the roof folds back neatly into the boot in about 20 seconds – 22 in fact, I think it is.

Tess Daly

Tess loved Culture Club in their 80s heyday, is fascinated by Japanese culture and has acquired a bit of a taste for posh polo events

Japan is the most incredible place in the whole world. While I was modelling, I was very fortunate to travel to some fantastic countries. I was getting paid for doing some amazing things, such as being in videos by Duran Duran, but nothing compares you for the culture shock that is Japan.

The writing of Wilbur Smith brought out the tomboy in me. I guess his stories were mainly for boys, but when I was young, I thought all the adventure stuff was terrific.

I'm a real high-street shopper at heart and Morgan is definitely my favourite shop. Even though I've been known to splash out up to £300 on a designer coat, I prefer Morgan because the designs are very trendy and great value for money.

I love Los Angeles and in particular Malibu, which is an amazing beachside community nearby. I was lucky enough to be there filming LA Pool Party with Lisa Snowdon and Jayne Middlemiss. Some of the sights you see and people you meet in Malibu are truly unbelievable.

I'm quite a keen Manchester United supporter. I have to say that I feel proud that so many of England's best international players play their league football at Old Trafford. The stadium is a wonderful place to watch football, although I'm more likely to support the team from the comfort of my armchair.

Opium by Yves Saint Laurent was the first perfume I really fell in love with. I must have been about 15 or so and, even though it smells beautiful, it's rather strong. My friends always used to joke that they could smell me coming.

I've been a bit of a polo fan ever since I attended a Cartier Polo event. All that champagne, flash cars, celebrity spotting and the beautiful ponies make for a great day out.

I grew up loving Culture Club and I'm lucky enough to have met Boy George, who's just hilarious. But it really all started because I had a huge crush on the gorgeous drummer Jon Moss. I even had posters of him all over my bedroom wall!

Sting

Sting, aka ex-teacher Gordon Sumner, is keen on yoga, admires Bruce Springsteen, loves South America and grows organic food

I wrote the song An Englishman In New York about Quentin Crisp because I really liked him a lot. He embodied a feminine ethic that I found very attractive. It wasn't sexual, but he was a very gentle, polite, well-mannered and giving person.

When I first took up yoga, I thought it was going to be all about old ladies in leotards. As a work-out, it's incredibly intense. It's not a cosmic experience at all. I'm definitely more supple now than I was at 21 and I can do things with my body I could never do at that age.

Maggie Thatcher still raises deep passions in me whenever I see her on TV. When she was in power, she believed people without money could just go to the wall. By using unemployment to keep inflation down she threw a generation down the drain, wasting their talent and energy.

Like almost everyone else from my home town, I'm a passionate Newcastle United supporter. It's weird in this business – years ago I was at Wembley watching England play and somebody came up to me and shook my hand because I was from the same city as Gazza. Geordies are so proud of their football heroes.

I'm really into organic food. If we have visitors, our Italian chef will normally prepare a dish using food grown on our organic farm, which is regularly vetted by inspectors from the Soil Association.

I love South America – it's such an interesting place. I feel at home whenever I'm there. The people, the literature, the music, environmental issues, religion, economics and the politics all fascinate me.

I've always been intrigued by the sea. It was the backdrop to my upbringing near the shipyards. It's been a recurring theme, dominating my memories and imagination.

Bruce Springsteen is a real hero of mine and also one of my closest friends. I first got to know him well when we both played on an Amnesty International world tour in 1988. Now we have a great time whenever we get together for a drink or a chat.

Tina O'Brien

When I was a kid, I loved the Ant And Dec Show on BBC1. They had this game called Beat The Barber. Contestants who answered questions wrongly had their hair hacked off by a real barber. Ant and Dec are brilliant.

The Velveteen Rabbit by Margery Williams makes me cry. It's the story of a toy rabbit who wants to become real and eventually manages to do so. It's really sad and moving. My mum read it to me when I was six and I just cried all the way through it. But I loved it so much, I soon learned to read it on my own.

My all-time favourite song is Build Me Up Buttercup by The Foundations. It's an old song, but a really happy tune that reminds me of my best friend Andrew. Both of us first heard it in the film There's Something About Mary and we used to dance around to it all the time.

The smell of Chanel No 5 brings back memories of when I was about eight. A friend of my nanna's used to get these little bottles for me and I'd dress up, put on lipstick and Chanel No 5 and pretend I was all grown up and posh. I suppose it was great practice for my acting career.

I've always loved seeing the Boddingtons ads. I think it's because I'm from Manchester. I loved the one in which the girl uses beer froth as face cream and when they went down the Manchester Ship Canal on a gondola as if it was Venice.

Friends is one of my favourite shows. Chandler is the best character because he's so adorable. I read an interview in which actor Matthew Perry says Chandler's personality was an exaggeration of his own, which I think is really sweet.

I'm totally into Big Brother. I've been watching it religiously and even tried to follow it on the internet. Even so, I wouldn't want to go on it myself.

Joseph And His Amazing Technicolor Dreamcoat with Phillip Schofield is the best musical I've ever seen. I saw it when I was nine and I was so envious of the kids on the stage. It made me decide I wanted to be an actress, so I started drama lessons.

Vanessa-Mae

Violinist Vanessa-Mae Nicholson loves skiing and going snorkelling. She also admits to a passion for caviar

I love my Casio altimeter watch. I'm sure there are more expensive and petite watches for girls, but I just adore my funky Casio.

If I had the chance of a free holiday, I'd rush back to the island of Nakatchafushi in the Maldives. I had a snorkelling holiday there when I was little and I found it hard to sleep at night because I kept dreaming of the multicoloured fish swimming towards me.

I'm a total skiing fanatic. I once treated myself to a skiing trip in Argentina, which was one of the most exhilarating things I've ever done – amazing! I'm quite an experienced skier these days because I've been doing it since I was young.

The Bible's my favourite book. If I were stranded on a desert island, it would be the ideal companion and also keep alive my dreams of being rescued.

My favourite author is Tom Sharpe – I think he's a genius. I especially love his book Porterhouse Blue and absolutely adored the TV adaptation of it starring David Jason.

Caviar is a great extravagance of mine. I eat the stuff by the spoonful, especially beluga caviar.

I share my birthday with Nicolò Paganini, who's my favourite composer. He was born in 1782 and was probably the greatest violin virtuoso ever. He was even lucky enough to play a Stradivarius.

Even though he comes in for a lot of criticism from the media, I still think Michael Jackson has amazing talent. If you go back and listen to the albums Thriller and Off The Wall, you'll know what I mean.

I just love Asia and Asian culture – it's so vibrant and full of energy. It's too tropical for me, though. I don't like the heat and I definitely don't like the humidity.

I have a passion for shoes. For years, I've been wearing slinky outfits with chunky shoes – I used to live in Buffalos. But now I'm venturing down Bond Street in London – I bought my first pair of Gina shoes there. I also love Versace shoes because they fit me really well.

Mick Hucknall

There's a side of Mick we don't often see – he loves cooking and doing Frank Spencer impersonations

I'm a real Grand Prix enthusiast and am fortunate enough to consider Damon Hill a good friend. It's an unbelievable feeling watching the cars racing around the circuit at such incredible speeds.

I was 11 when I bought my first album, Sticky Fingers by The Rolling Stones. They're the greatest rock 'n' roll band of all time and always will be. No one can get near them and Keith Richards is the most underrated guitar player.

Little Richard is a real hero of mine – he has an energy that's just so intense. I first heard him when I was a teenager and his music seemed to have a real madness about it. You could see it in his eyes. Can you imagine what effect it would have had on concerned parents in the 50s?

As a kid, I used to really enjoy doing impersonations. Like a lot of people at the time, I often did Frank Spencer impressions. I'm still an addictive mimic. I just can't help it.

As a lifelong Labour supporter, I first met Tony Blair at the 1992 Brit Awards. He's a good bloke. I helped fund his campaign for the party leadership and I think he's one of this century's great leaders.

I first met Robert De Niro in Milan a few years back and we really hit it off. He's very funny off screen and, obviously, I love his acting, particularly when he speaks Italian in The Godfather 2.

I'm very much pro-European and have a tattoo of the European flag. I think federalism must be handled sensibly, though, and that there should still be cultural independence within each country.

I support Manchester United. I've been going to Old Trafford for as long as I can remember.

When I'm in Italy, I love staying at home to cook spaghetti al pomodoro e basilico, which is probably my favourite dish. When I first went to live in Milan, I took all my spices with me from Manchester because they don't have Indian spices. In fact, there aren't any Indian restaurants in Milan at all.

Vanessa Paradis

Shopping in Parisian markets and going to the Notting Hill Carnival are Vanessa's idea of a good time

Les Puces de Clignancourt is a flea market in Paris where I love to hang out. I like to buy classic second-hand clothes there or just meet friends for a coffee. I prefer 70s styles. Clothes shopping for me is an obsession.

As a child, I always had posters of Marilyn Monroe on my walls, especially from Gentleman Prefer Blondes. I've read countless biographies about her tragic life, but I think she still manages to be an inspiration to many women.

Chanel is a magical product in France and I've always admired Coco Chanel. I've worn Chanel No 5 for years — it's definitely my favourite perfume. I wear it because Marilyn Monroe was once asked what she wore in bed and she replied 'Chanel No 5'.

London's Notting Hill Carnival is my kind of party. I loved it when I saw Jazzy B DJ-ing with his Soul II Soul sound system. It's a really carefree celebration of life and music. I often wish I'd been a hippy in the 60s with flowers in my hair.

Lenny Kravitz is one of the most talented musicians in the world. He's one of the funniest human beings, too. He's very intense to work with. We were like twins when he played on my album — no one can touch him.

Jamaica's my favourite place. The people there have a wonderful, laid-back attitude to life.

I love Labradors because, even though they're big dogs, they have such a friendly nature. I once looked after a friend's for six months, but then someone stole it, which really upset me and my friend.

I really love Vivienne Westwood's clothes. She's like an artist who uses history as her inspiration. Her famous basques are reminiscent of the way the French aristocracy dressed 200 years ago. She's a genius.

Boyz N The Hood is a great film and I first saw it in Los Angeles. The next day, I was shopping and I saw the cops arrest these two black guys with guns, like a scene from the film. It was really crazy, but my friend just said: 'Ah, it's nothing. It's just LA.'

Lenny Henry

Lenny's heroes include Stevie Wonder, Nelson Mandela and Richard Pryor. The comedian was awarded a CBE in 1999

Woody Allen's Manhattan is one of those movies I can watch again and again – it just seems the perfect little film to me. It looks beautiful, the performances are incredibly well-judged and Woody's very funny in it. The opening sequence alone is worth the entrance fee.

Richard Pryor was one of my favourite comedians. He developed multiple sclerosis – but he led an incredible life and I salute his bravery. At his peak, he was the funniest man in the world. He was a very big influence on me.

I bought Stevie Wonder's Songs In The Key Of Life in 1976 and kept it in its wrapper for two weeks until I had time to listen to it properly. It blew my head off – it was wonderful. I've still got the album, but now I've got it on CD.

I love West Indian food but, if I'm really honest, some of the best nights I've ever had have been in an Indian restaurant or eating Indian food at my house. I like everything really, especially baltis, but if I had to pick a favourite dish, it would be a lamb balti with a big naan bread. Just perfect.

I greatly admire Nelson Mandela for the fortitude and dignity with which he served his 28-year jail sentence. I've met him twice and was astounded by how many tiny wrinkles he has. I felt that they illustrated just how much time had been stolen from him. But he still had a big smile on his face.

I loved watching Thunderbirds as a child – the entire Henry family would sit down of an evening and watch it together. They put it on at 7pm – I can't think of a children's show that they'd do that with now. I remember all the catch phrases and I liked Lady Penelope and Parker. Theirs was a strange relationship.

The first series of BBC1's The Lakes was perfect TV. I'd love to work with its writer, Jimmy McGovern, because he has major things to say about the human condition. I enjoyed the second series, too, although I did miss his writing. Still, I thought the new writers did very well indeed.

Zoë Ball

Zoë dents her 'ladette' image by confessing to a weakness for ultra-feminine Italian fashion, cleaning the house and having a schoolgirl crush on Phillip Schofield

At music festivals I enjoy some serious moshing, which means really wild dancing at the front of the stage. I like to get a bit muddy and Glastonbury is great because all that rain just brings out the Dunkirk spirit. I don't just stay in the VIP areas at these events.

As a schoolgirl, I had a huge crush on Pip – sorry – Phillip Schofield. He kissed me on my cheek when I was 15 and I didn't wash for a week! He was the Des Lynam of Saturday morning TV. I used to watch Sally James on Tiswas as well – she was really cool.

I loved the Ford Ka when it came out because when I was a little girl, it was exactly how I imagined a car in the year 2000 would look. It was brilliant for a city girl like me, even though the clampers of Camden took a shine to it as well and it cost me a small fortune.

I have a bit of a designer fetish. It got to the point where I was shopping at Prada so often, they'd open the door for me if they saw me crossing the street. I really love Italian fashion. I once bought a pair of £300 Dolce & Gabanna boots and wore them only once. Is that bad?

I've always found Terence Stamp very sexy. Especially in the late 60s when he was living with Michael Caine and going out with the stunning Jean Shrimpton. Oh, he's tall, too. I've never fancied short blokes.

I went to Havana on holiday once and it's an amazing place. I drank far too many rum and Cokes when I was there and did lots of dancing on tables. Cubans love to dance and salsa music is so sexy, too.

Woody Allen is a genius. He's quite sexy in a cerebral way, too. My favourite films of his are Love And Death, Annie Hall and Play It Again, Sam. I love the way he captures New York on film – it's such an amazing city anyway.

Cleaning the house is my absolute favourite pastime. I love putting on very loud music and really attacking the toilet, the bath and the fridge. You name it, I'll scrub it. But I have to be wearing my yellow Marigold gloves, size medium.

Linford Christie

Former Olympic 100m champion Linford is a fan of South Park and kung fu, but doesn't have a high opinion of footballers

If I had to choose one song that means the most to me, it would be I Believe I Can Fly by R Kelly. The lyrics are truly inspirational because I actually believed I could fly when I was running my races. Sprinting will always be my No 1 passion because it's a true sport.

I've been given a lot of free training shoes, but I was particularly fond of some suede trainers Puma sent me. I had every single colour of the rainbow.

I'm a very keen armchair Manchester United fan, but I've never been to a game in my life. That's because I think footballers, unlike athletes, are actors. They roll around on the floor trying to catch the eye of the referee.

The Queen And I by Sue Townsend is definitely the best book I've ever read. I probably reread it every few years because it just makes me laugh so much.

I go back to Jamaica as often as I can. I was born there and get treated like a celebrity whenever I visit. I love presenting awards at Jamaican athletics meetings or just hanging out with friends in Montego Bay.

Jodeci are a really melodic swingbeat group from America. They had a big hit here with a song called Freek'n You from an album entitled The Show, The After-Party, The Hotel. There's nothing better to play in your car.

I'm a huge fan of kung fu. I was never really into Bruce Lee, but Jackie Chan and another bloke called Jet Li are the real governors of the martial arts. I've got over 50 of their films.

South Park is brilliant. It's even better than The Simpsons because the humour's more adult.

I like to treat myself to a bottle of Issey Miyake. It's my favourite aftershave – but I always buy it in duty-free shops.

Face/Off is a great film. I'm a big fan of Nicolas Cage and also loved his movies The Rock and Con Air. He's not classically good-looking, but he does get all the funny lines.

Anna Friel

Anna loves Al Pacino, Cornwall's rugged coastline, shopping in New York, being totally pampered and the works of Charles Dickens

I used to smoke white-tip Marlboro Lights cigarettes. You can only get them in America. When I was in the US and I bought them, I always got told: 'Oh, honey, you're going to ruin your skin and you're so beautiful anyway – don't ruin it.' Now I've stopped.

Collette Dinnigan is my favourite designer. But I don't like wearing anything that exposes too much midriff because I hate my tummy.

I'd love to live in St Ives in Cornwall. The coastline gives you a feeling of true escapism. It's very easy for people in the media to get caught up in the whole London thing, but it really isn't that important and you should always try to enjoy Britain's wonderful countryside.

I once had my Tarot cards read when I was in New York. I'm not overly superstitious, but the card reading was surprisingly accurate.

I love Al Pacino. He's got absolutely everything – sex appeal, charisma, talent and elegance. I especially love him in Carlito's Way and Scent Of A Woman. If I could act opposite him, I'd probably be so overwhelmed, I'd faint.

I've always been a fan of Charles Dickens. The thing is, when you act in a Dickens drama, you can rehearse for three months and still have many different interpretations. That's how deep his writing is.

I eventually took up yoga after many years. I never knew how to unwind. I used to get home and continue to be a bit hyperactive, doing loads of things, and it took me years to learn how to chill out properly and find the time to relax.

The shopping in New York is amazing! And it seems so cheap. I would recommend anyone from England wanting to go on a shopping binge to go there for a weekend.

I love the pampering and beauty stuff that everyone does so regularly in New York – all the manicures and pedicures and massages. One of my favourite places is Bliss Spa. I love the fact that you can get a masseuse to come and visit your home.

196

Peter Stringfellow

Peter admires Errol Flynn and loves to hang out on his yacht with a plate of oysters

A bottle of chilled Pinot Grigio is the best way to unwind. It really gets you in the mood for love. Drink one of those babies and you're well on your way.

The most beautiful building can be found in the most beautiful city in the world. It's the marvellous Palace of Versailles just outside Paris. I couldn't wait to take my girlfriend to see it while we were in France for Valentine's Day.

When I'm not in London working, I live aboard my Camargue 50 Sunseeker yacht. It's the most wonderful boat to entertain friends on. I tend to sail between Majorca and Ibiza in the Balearic Islands.

Errol Flynn is my hero in terms of being a romantic leading man. He was perfect as Robin Hood as he summed up sex, adventure and basically just getting away with it. As a kid, we'd make jokes about his willy being at least a foot long.

My favourite film is Casablanca and that's why I sometimes have it playing on screens in my club. I love Humphrey Bogart's character because I am Rick! He was a bit ugly, but somehow always got the girl. There's something about him that women just adore.

My favourite smell on a girl is jasmine. My girlfriend knows that I love it when she puts it in my bath. She put too much in the other day, but that's another story. Jasmine blossom straight off the tree makes me feel quite heady.

The best love song of all time has got to be 10CC's I'm Not In Love. When it came out, it was the finest smoochy dance song around. And if you couldn't connect with a girl in your arms on the dance floor while it played in the background, then you were destined to never ever have a relationship.

Oysters really are the ultimate aphrodisiac. The ritual of eating them is such a sexual act. To do it properly, the man prepares the oyster and loosens it and then, still holding it, tilts the lady's head back and slides it down her throat.

Amanda Redman

Zanzibar is the most incredible place I've ever been to – it's so stunningly beautiful. The colours are wonderful and the people are brilliant. It's idyllic. It's also not all that well known, so you don't tend to get lots of tourists.

I'm a shoe-aholic – Jimmy Choo is my favourite. It's not just that the designs and the colours are so unusual and so beautiful – you can go to an arduous work event in six-inch heels and by the end of the evening your feet aren't hurting. The engineering is just perfect.

Katharine Hepburn was a great woman in every way. It wasn't just her acting ability, she was so modern in all her attitudes, really ahead of her time. The way she handled her relationship with Spencer Tracy with such dignity was so impressive.

Cigarettes are my main indulgence. I smoke Silk Cut. I do realise that I'm killing myself. Every time I've tried to stop, people say: 'For Christ's sake, start again – you're just horrible.' I've tried so many times, but it's just so difficult.

I adore curry – any kind. I eat it at least twice a week. I have been known to eat it every night, although I try not to do that. My favourite night in is to order a takeaway curry and watch a movie on TV.

Birdsong by Sebastian Faulks is one of those books that affected me profoundly. I adored it. I thought it was absolutely extraordinary. No other book has ever evoked the horror of war so well. If you haven't read it, you should.

I was walking through Selfridges once and someone sprayed me with Issey Miyake perfume. I thought it was beautiful because I really like lemony scents. That day, three people came up to me and asked me what perfume I was wearing, so I decided this was obviously the scent for me. I love it.

Brief Encounter never ceases to make me weep. I watch it over and over again and I cry every time. It's the bit when Celia Johnson gets home and is talking to her husband. That's the bit that always gets me. It's one of the best films ever made.

Ronan Keating

Singer Ronan is a huge fan of actor Gary Oldman and his biggest ambition is to play Batman in a film

Gary Oldman is a fabulous actor, especially when he takes on really intense roles. I loved him in State Of Grace in which he played opposite Sean Penn and Ed Harris. It's definitely one of my all-time favourite films because it examines the role of the Irish Mafia in New York.

Rowan Atkinson is a genius. It was a fantastic experience making the video of the single Picture Of You for the Mr Bean movie because, instead of using a script, he just made up all the movements as he went along. The result was hilarious and we almost wet ourselves laughing.

When I visited Tokyo for the first time, I was stunned by how much it reminded me of Gotham City in the Batman movies. I've always been a huge fan of the caped crusader, a character I would love to play in a movie one day.

Playing golf is one of my biggest passions. I'm a member of my local club and the Irish professional Christy O'Connor Jr has even given me a few lessons. I've also played with Scottish pro Colin Montgomerie but, luckily, I don't feel intimidated being with golfers of that calibre. You just hope to pick up the odd tip on your swing.

I'm really into barbecuing food these days. In fact, you could almost call me Mr Barbecue! I find it really therapeutic and it takes my mind off work. Marinated chicken or steaks are my speciality.

Since I was a kid, I've dreamed of owning a Harley-Davidson motorbike and riding across America with the wind blowing in my face and the sun on my back. At least now I'm halfway there because I own one. Riding it is one of the greatest thrills in the world.

I'm into rallying big time. Cars have always been a passion of mine. My brother used to be a car mechanic, so from a young age I was into the whole thing. I love the idea of being in control, of being able to master a car and understand it.

I went to see Take That recently. It was great. I have to say it was one of the most entertaining shows I've ever been to. They were amazing.

Alicia Silverstone

Alicia says she finds meditation wonderfully relaxing and enjoys collecting teapots

I find meditation a wonderful way to relax. In my business you need time to reflect and cleanse your mind. I feel so refreshed after I have meditated. I am ready to face the day, whatever it may bring.

Thanksgiving is a wonderful time in our house. We celebrate the love we have for each other. It's a massive vegan celebration with all our family and friends – just a huge love festival.

I watch the TV series 24 religiously – it's so exciting, with lots of twists. My idea of a perfect evening is curling up on the couch watching Kiefer Sutherland saving the world on TV.

As a kid, I watched The Wizard Of Oz over and over again. It's a fun movie and I could never get enough of it. I loved the opening title sequence – it was so exciting.

I'm a devoted vegan – it's such a healthy way to live without hurting any living creature. My favourite dish is home-made vegetable soup. It makes me feel all warm and cosy when I eat it.

My favourite movie is Frank Capra's Mr Smith Goes To Washington, which was released in 1939. It's aged so well and the performances from Jimmy Stewart and Jean Arthur are superb. I love it a bit more every time I watch it.

I absolutely adore dogs and I've adopted four. I found my eldest, Samson, wandering the streets of LA and I just had to give him a home. They all have their own personalities and bring me so much joy.

The Amazon is the most amazing river in the world. It's so big – more than 4,000 miles long – and surrounded by the rainforest. I truly feel at peace there.

I have a large collection of teapots. Both my parents are British and every time I see my mum she brings me a new one. I'm not usually a collector of things, but I am getting very fond of them.

I'm a complete yoga addict. I live quite a healthy lifestyle, but I don't think I'd feel so good if I was on some crazy diet.

Index